Experiencing
the Power
of Healing
Prayer

HOW TO PRAY
WHEN LIFE
HURTS

Roy Lawrence

INTERVARSITY PRESS
DOWNERS GROVE, ILLINOIS 60515

InterVarsity Press® is the book-publishing division of InterVarsity Christian Fellowship®, a student movement active on campus at hundreds of universities, colleges and schools of nursing in the United States of America, and a member movement of the International Fellowship of Evangelical Students. For information about local and regional activities, write Public Relations Dept., Inter-Varsity Christian Fellowship, 6400 Schroeder Rd., P.O. Box 7895, Madison, WI 53707-7895.

Scripture quotations, unless otherwise noted, are from the New Revised Standard Version of the Bible, copyright 1989 by the Division of Christian Education of the National Council of the Churches of Christ in the U.S.A. and are used by permission.

Cover photograph: Daryl Benson

ISBN 0-8308-1384-5

Printed in the United States of America ∞

Library of Congress Cataloging-in-Publication Data

Lawrence, Roy, 1931-
   How to pray when life hurts: experiencing the power of healing
prayer/Roy Lawrence.
     p.   cm.
   ISBN 0-8308-1384-5
   1. Prayer—Christianity. 2. Spiritual healing.   I. Title.
BV227.L396 1993
248.3'2—dc20

                                             92-35136
                                              CIP

15	14	13	12	11	10	9	8	7	6	5	4
03	02	01	00	99	98	97					

Acknowledgments

I am grateful to all who have made this book possible. My colleagues and congregation at St. Stephen's, Prenton, shared in a two-year School of Prayer that provided the basic material I present here. Andrew Le Peau and his editorial team at Inter-Varsity Press offered many helpful suggestions. My wife, Eira, read each chapter carefully and made important contributions to both content and style. One of my parishioners, Joan Butterworth, undertook the considerable task of typing my manuscript.

I dedicate this book to my colleagues in the Acorn Christian Healing Trust, who, under the leadership of Bishop Morris Maddocks (adviser to the archbishops of Canterbury and York in the Ministry of Christian Healing), are working so hard and so imaginatively to seek to restore the healing gospel to Britain.

Roy Lawrence

Prayer is a key

which unlocks the

blessings of the day

and locks up the dangers

of the night.

[ANONYMOUS]

—ONE—

THE HEALING POWER OF PRAYER

*T*he Bible makes extraordinary claims for the healing power of prayer. Jesus said, "Very truly, I tell you, the one who believes in me will also do the works that I do and, in fact, will do greater works than these, because I am going to the Father. I will do whatever you ask in my name, so that the Father may be glorified in the Son. If in my name you ask me for anything, I will do it" (Jn 14:12-14).

Do we believe a word of this? It is a remarkable claim! Jesus says that where bodies and minds are racked by pain, he can make a difference. He always did during his earthly ministry, and he still can—in fact, more so, because the Holy Spirit reaches across a much wider geographical area than Jesus could encompass during his years on earth.

Where lives and attitudes have gone wrong, Jesus can make a difference there. Even when, in human terms, a situation is beyond hope—when a marriage has come to the point of total breakdown, when a cancer has been diagnosed as incurable, when an addiction is out of control—it is never beyond the reach of Jesus, never beyond the healing difference Christ can make.

Prayer is the key. James says, "The prayer of faith will save the sick, and the Lord will raise them up; and anyone who has committed sins will be forgiven. Therefore confess your sins to one another, and pray for one another, so that you may be healed" (Jas 5:15-16).

But when did you last have a lesson in prayer? Was it in childhood—perhaps in Sunday school?

A rough, tough sergeant-major once assured me, "There are no atheists on a battlefield. When you think your life is in danger, you pray—everybody prays." When I asked him what sort of prayer he had prayed on the battlefield, he looked rather embarrassed and said, "Gentle Jesus, meek and mild, look upon a little child." It was the prayer of a four-year-old; he hadn't had any prayer instruction since early childhood!

Christian churches are good at telling us that we *ought* to pray, but not nearly so good at telling us how. In my parish, we have recently learned a great deal by sharing in a "School of Prayer." It lasted for two years, during which we came together once a month to learn more about the prayer that heals. Since then I have had the privilege of leading schools of prayer in many other churches and groups.

We know that prayer does heal—at any rate, some of the time. As I write these words, examples come flooding into my mind. I think of a little boy with a seemingly unrestrainable impulse toward violence. He wrecked the house and terrorized his sister and even his mother. Yet after prayer in the name of Jesus, he was changed; he quieted down and has been a much calmer child ever since. Somehow the violence was driven out of him.

I think of a woman who had been crippled by multiple sclerosis; two weeks after she received prayer in the name of Jesus, she was able to leave her wheelchair and even to ride her bicycle again. I think of another woman who was afflicted with cancer and on the verge of death—so her doctor told me. But after she received prayer in Jesus' name, a hospital x-ray showed that the cancer had totally disappeared.

Even when miracles seem in very short supply, when emotional problems remain unresolved or a tumor does not shrink, prayer is never wasted. I can think of many times when the specific healings I've prayed for have not materialized, but the situation changed in other ways. These, too, are answers to prayer. Later in this book I'll offer some examples.

Attitudes and relationships can change after prayer. Problems can become unexpected opportunities. A dimension of healing can be brought into the experience of death itself. In such situations it would be wrong to say that there was no healing.

Prayer can make a difference, because Jesus makes a difference. But it has to be the real Jesus, and it has to be real prayer. So often our prayer is a hit-and-miss affair. We have not matured as men and women of prayer because we have not put a fraction of the time, thought and effort into learning to pray which we readily invest in our work, our hobbies, our human relationships. So it is that grown-up people who wouldn't dream of filling their stomachs with baby food or filling their conversation with baby talk are still babies—untaught, unpracticed, immature—in the all-important art of prayer.

If we are retarded in prayer, then we ourselves suffer for it—but so does the world. The world needs us to be prayer therapists. Prayer is God's appointed way by which we become channels of his healing power.

In our parish prayer school, we have studied methods of prayer, practiced them together and shared our findings and our feelings with each other. With this book we invite you to be our companions on the way of prayer. As you read on, may God bless you and make you a blessing to others through prayer.

If you, O LORD, should

mark iniquities,

Lord, who could stand?

But there is forgiveness with you,

so that you may be revered.

[PSALM 130:3-4]

HOW DO YOU PRAY WHEN YOU FEEL GUILTY OR ASHAMED?

*C*hristian healing is concerned with the entire spectrum of life. It's concerned with body, mind and spirit, with attitudes and relationships, with lifestyles and life situations, with time and eternity. It is extended not only to individuals but also to neighborhoods and even nations.

Just as Jesus was born into a specific time and situation, so our prayers must be tailor-made for the way things are and the way we ourselves are at *this moment.*

God is always the same, but we are not. We have good days

and bad days. We are capable of an infinite number of reactions to life. A prayer method that is right and proper when we are on top of the world is not necessarily appropriate when we are close to despair.

The Bible gives us examples of this. The psalmists certainly had their "praise-the-Lord" days, but they also had their "I-am-poor-and-in-misery" days, and their approach to prayer differed accordingly.

Healing prayer always involves coming into the presence of God, but it has to be *the real me* that I bring into his presence. He can do all kinds of things with the real me, however out of sorts I may feel, but he can do nothing at all with a bogus, pseudo-pious self. Unreal prayers will do no good for me or for anyone else. Our motto needs to be "Just as I am, I come."

In our parish school of prayer, one of our basic aims has been to look honestly at common states of mind and discover how we can bring them to God.

For instance—how do you pray when you feel guilty or ashamed?

I hope we all do feel guilty and ashamed from time to time. I know that some guilt feelings are false, neurotic and thoroughly undesirable. For example, if we have suffered deep wrongs but choose to bottle up and repress our feelings of anger, we may find that those feelings turn in on us. In that case, what actually comes into our conscious mind is a disproportionate sense of guilt. We find ourselves obsessively worrying about some tiny or even nonexistent sin.

I will deal with this type of unhealthy guilt in my next chapter. Here, though, I want to point out that a certain amount of guilt and shame is good and healthy and realistic, because we are all sinners; we all break God's laws. Guilt is one reason we need Jesus' healing.

"All have sinned and fall short of the glory of God," says Paul (Rom 3:23). The evidence is all around us. We switch on the TV to watch the news, and the evidence pours out. We open the daily paper, and there it is again. We belong to a world in trouble, and we would be quite conceited and out of touch with reality if we supposed that it was all other people's fault.

Yet we *can* delude ourselves into the assumption that we are blameless, and some people do so. We can take out the psychological whitewash brush and slap it all over ourselves. We can be like the Pharisee who said, "God, I thank you that I am not like other people" (Lk 18:11).

When in my first parish I had the temerity to preach on the universality of sin, an influential woman in the village swept out of the sanctuary afterward and addressed me sternly: "Young man, I would have you know that I for one am perfectly pure!"

I wrote a poem once about a man who persuaded himself that everything wrong was somebody else's fault:

When Johnny was four
If he broke a toy
He always blamed
Another boy.
To get in trouble seemed a shame
If someone else could take the blame.

Now John is a man
And the world is brim
full of folly
And full of sin,

So Johnny goes out and looks to see
Just who the guilty men can be.

He blames the great.
He blames the small.
Jews—blacks—reds—
He blames them all.
In fact, there really is only one
He doesn't blame. Guess who? It's John!

It is much more wholesome and realistic to admit that we are part of the world's troubles. The human race has gone wrong—and that includes us. Honest prayer requires honest self-assessment. It includes self-examination, testing ourselves according to standards provided by God.

The Ten Commandments provide a useful measure for life. I have listed them here for your reflection, adding some questions to help you work out the underlying implications of each one.

1. I am the LORD your God. . . . you shall have no other gods before me. Do I worship God regularly and sincerely? Do I love him? Do I trust him? Do I seek to obey him? If so, what are the practical signs of this in my life? And if God is important to me, do I help others to know him and worship him?

2. You shall not make for yourself an idol. Many think they are free from idolatry because they do not have a golden calf in the backyard! But they may be sadly mistaken. Idolatry can take many forms. Is there anything I love more than God? Then I turn it into my idol. Money perhaps? Popularity? Possessions? Power? Myself? Some other person? Some secret sin?

3. You shall not make wrongful use of the name of the LORD your God. Some think that blasphemy is an insignificant little sin, hardly worthy of attention, but it can damage us and our society because often the mind follows the mouth. If we speak casually about holy things, we may find ourselves thinking casually about them and living casually. So do I reverence God in my thoughts? In my words? In my life? Do I take care about the sorts of TV programs I watch and the kinds of magazines I read?

4. Remember the sabbath day, and keep it holy. In the book of Exodus, breaking the sabbath is regarded as a crime so great that it actually merits the death penalty (Ex 31:15)! If that seems extreme, it does remind us that a society that discards its holy day is taking a first step to losing its soul. When material things crowd out spiritual things, watch out. The person who is too busy for God is just too busy! So do I keep the Lord's Day for worship, prayer and recreation?

5. Honor your father and your mother. A society that scorns older people is sowing the seeds of the destruction of family life. We do this at our peril. So do I love, respect and help my parents? Also, bearing in mind that the Christian church can be considered my spiritual mother, do I honor my church and act as its faithful son or daughter? And what about the country that gave me birth? Do I honor my country and fulfill my duties as a citizen?

6. You shall not murder. We may breathe a sigh of relief at this point—here, at any rate, is a commandment we do not break. But what about murder by neglect? The rich man in the story Jesus told is guilty of it when he neglects the poor man at his gate and lets him die (Lk 16:19-31). Are we similarly guilty? While one-third of the world's population is overfed, two-thirds goes hungry. Many die of hunger. What am I doing to prevent these needless deaths? Do I support ministries and organizations that fight famine?

And what about mental murder or character assassination? Do I bear any grudge or hatred in my heart? Have I injured anyone by my words or deeds? Do I promote peace, or do I act as a troublemaker? Am I courteous? Am I kind to all God's creatures?

7. *You shall not commit adultery.* Sexual purity is important. In Leviticus 20, many forms of impurity are assigned the death penalty (see vv. 10, 13 and 15). If that seems extreme, remember that with the advent of AIDS sexual behavior has become a matter of life and death. So am I clean in thought, word and deed? Am I the master of my bodily desires, or am I their slave? Am I faithful to my marriage vows?

8. *You shall not steal.* Am I honest and fair in all I do? Or do I practice some form of dishonesty? Perhaps conventional dishonesty, telling myself that everybody does it? Or petty dishonesty, on the grounds that nobody will notice?

Have I stolen praise or credit that does not belong to me? Or look at Malachi 3:8-9—if you dare: "Will anyone rob God?" asks Malachi. The answer seems obvious, rhetorical: of course not. Yet Malachi tells us we do rob God when we fail to give God his due "tithes and offerings" from our income. The prophet offers us these words from God, and they echo ominously across the centuries: "You are cursed with a curse, for you are robbing me—the whole nation of you!" So does enough of my money, my time and my energy go back to God by the way I give and the way I live?

9. *You shall not bear false witness.* Here we come back to the concept of character assassination. Have I ever told a lie in order to hurt someone? Do I spread harmful gossip? Do I listen to harmful gossip? Have I ever by my silence allowed anyone to be wrongly condemned?

10. *You shall not covet.* We will be looking at this later when

we ask, "How do you pray when you feel jealous and envious?" But for now, can I identify the sin of covetousness in my life? Or—putting it more positively—am I able to be happy about the good fortune of others? When I am fortunate myself, does it make me thankful to God and generous to the people around me?

My guess is that each of the Ten Commandments pricks each of us at one time or another. If they do not get us sooner, they get us later. And a good thing too! Just as a doctor cannot prescribe until he or she has diagnosed, so a good "prayer prescription" is dependent upon an accurate diagnosis of our basic spiritual condition.

If this method of diagnosis for some reason does not speak to you personally, you might try 1 Corinthians 13:4-7 as an alternative, changing the statements about love into personal questions—"Am I patient? Kind? Do I know no envy? Do I avoid boasting? Am I never arrogant? Never rude? Do I never insist on my own way? Am I never irritable? Never resentful? Am I never glad when others go wrong? Am I gladdened by the truth? Am I always slow to expose? Always eager to believe the best? Always hopeful? Always patient?"

Or even more simply, in your imagination you can stand beside Jesus, who represents everything that human life is meant to be. How do you feel?

If you feel guilty and ashamed, then perhaps the first word I should speak to you is "congratulations." There is absolutely no merit in self-deception, complacency and conceit. It is much better to admit the truth and see ourselves as we are.

After honestly admitting our guilt, the second step toward getting right with God is to tell him we are sorry. Admission of the facts and penitence for our sins do not necessarily go together. It is perfectly possible to see things exactly as they are but be quite brazen about it. Only when diagnosis develops into repentance can we take the next step toward our healing.

Our prayer life is not complete unless we are sorry for our sins and we want to change and we tell God so. Sometimes we will find ourselves discussing our sins with him in detail. Sometimes we will be brief about it. It is rather like cleaning a house. Sometimes a flick with a duster will do, but at other times we need a deep spring cleaning.

We need to say, "Lord, I have looked carefully at myself, and I do acknowledge the unpleasant truths I have found out about myself," and then, "Lord, I am truly sorry for the ways I have failed you, failed other people and failed my own best self." Then we are ready for our third step—the step that takes us to the foot of the cross, where Jesus died that we might be forgiven. This, for the Christian, is the most important step in the world.

Here is a prayer for any who may need help in taking that step.

Jesus, I know that I am a sinner, and I'm truly sorry for the wrongs I have done, but I also know that you love me and gave yourself for me. You offer to come into my life if I will let you in. You offer healing for the sins and hurts of my soul. You offer to feed me with your own truth.

Gratefully I accept your offer to be my Savior, Lord and Friend. I ask for forgiveness. I put my trust in you and want you at work in me, healing me, feeding me, living in me.

Help me to use my life in your service. Thank you for all you are going to do in me. Amen.

We use a similar prayer again and again at our parish healing services, and I believe that as the worshipers make it their own, the miracle of forgiveness takes place. Christ offers sinners like us a healing and saving relationship, and he himself pays the price to make it possible. There is extraordinary life-transforming power in the cross. As he hangs there, Jesus loves us in spite of the pain our sinfulness has caused him. This is the heart of forgiveness: not ignoring what has been done or pretending that wrong is right, but seeing things just as they are and yet going on loving and paying the price.

As the miracle of forgiveness takes place, the way is clear for us to take one further step in prayer, which is to say thank you for our costly forgiveness and to begin to enjoy the freedom that forgiveness brings.

The apostle John says, "If we say that we have no sin, we deceive ourselves, and the truth is not in us." But, he goes on, "if we confess our sins, he who is faithful and just will forgive us our sins and cleanse us from all unrighteousness" (1 Jn 1:8-9).

So then, how do you pray when you feel guilty or ashamed? Admit the facts without deception. Tell God you are sorry. Ask for forgiveness in the name of Jesus. Accept the forgiveness Jesus offers, and enjoy the release and healing he brings.

Incidentally, you may find this prayer-sequence is not only mentally and spiritually liberating but physically liberating as well. Many physical conditions can have an element of unresolved guilt at their root.

I know a dermatologist who prays forgiveness prayers with her patients if normal medical healing procedures seem not to work. She says these prayers are sometimes amazingly effective.

I myself remember a woman with an unpleasant skin rash that actually vanished before my eyes when she accepted God's forgiveness for a past sin. Body, mind and spirit are all mysteriously interconnected. Our God has great plans for all three!

Suffering, particularly where it is

the result of injustice or where it occurs

through no fault of the victim, can

lead to anger and bitterness. It can easily

block off the flow of practical trust

in God. Such pain needs to be expressed.

[ROWLAND CROUCHER]

THREE

HOW DO YOU PRAY WHEN YOU ARE ANGRY OR DEPRESSED?

*M*any people harbor a great deal of anger deep inside. Anger plays a much bigger part in life than we generally recognize. One of the clues to this fact is that anybody running a discussion group has only to ask the question, "What in the world irritates you most?" and suddenly everyone will have something to say, no matter how sluggishly the discussion has flowed up to that point.

Sometimes anger is openly expressed. TV cameras can pick it up on the furious faces of rioters, strikers or demonstrators.

Sometimes it is only partly expressed. The sharpest part of our anger can be pushed under the surface, so that what actually shows itself is resentment rather than rage, a tendency to cherish grudges, a "chip on the shoulder," smoldering embers rather than a blazing fire.

Sometimes anger can be completely repressed. This means that though it is present, it is not shown or felt. The man who is repressing anger may wear an apologetic smile on his face, but that does not mean that his anger has ceased to exist. It means that it has buried itself in the subconscious mind. From this hiding place it will wage a sort of guerrilla warfare, both on its host and on the world at large.

Repressed anger can damage the human spirit in many ways. It is one of the commonest causes of depression. That's why this chapter addresses both anger and depression.

The person who harbors repressed anger will often feel weighed down by real, or imaginary, troubles. Joy will be excluded. Life will be seen as a burdensome set of requirements. Even the Christian faith will be thought of in terms of rules and regulations rather than as a way of healing and liberation. Also, as I mentioned in the last chapter, there can be a growth of debilitating neurotic guilt, which is immune to rational discussion or to the assurance of forgiveness.

Repressed anger does not only harm the spirit. It harms the body too. The hidden struggle going on in the subconscious mind results in a lack of energy and concentration. The depressed person can be exhausted and yet quite unable to sleep. Although the anger is unconscious, the nervous system is still activated for a fight. So the head may be tense, the heartbeat rapid and irregular, the muscles taut, the stomach tight. Repressed anger can be a factor in an assortment of ailments. If a patient has a tendency to asthma, repressed anger can activate it—and anger can also aggravate a tendency to arthritis. It can block up the system, causing congestion at one end or constipation at the other!

Also, because the anger is not dealt with but merely stored, it will likely erupt from time to time in a totally irrational way— as in the case of the man who is compelled to humble himself before his boss at work, concealing all his anger, but then finds himself going home, snapping at his wife, shouting at the children and kicking the cat. Sometimes the anger can erupt not against others but against self. It can do a U-turn, producing strong suicidal feelings.

If the repression of anger is so dangerous, why is it so common? For one thing, nice people are not at ease expressing anger. Perhaps our parents and teachers worked hard to make sure we knew that the polite and socially respectable thing is to keep anger under control. If we do not know how to get rid of anger, we have to put it into cold storage deep inside, where it becomes a frozen, heavy, uncomfortable, dispiriting lump.

There is a further factor that leads us to keep our anger out of sight—and many people find this a totally devastating thought. Much anger is really directed not against human beings, but against God. He made us and put us into a world that is quite beautiful but can also be bewildering and painful. We are taught that God is our protector and defender, yet he may not have prevented others from harming us.

If we are honest, our feelings toward God will not always be dutiful and grateful and subservient. Sometimes, perhaps buried under a conventionally pious exterior, there is a concealed snake pit of hissing, seething rage against our Creator.

In chapter eleven of my earlier book *Christian Healing Rediscovered,* I told the story of Greg, a bottled-up, angry man. The name (as in all the case histories I use for illustrative purposes) was a false one, but the situation was true and typical of many others.

Greg presented many of the physical and mental symptoms of repressed anger. His head felt tense. He could not breathe properly because of continual nasal congestion. He had a tight feeling in his chest, and his heart beat irregularly. He perspired continually. By night he could not sleep; by day he could not concentrate. His nails were bitten down. He looked as though he were trying to carry the weight of the world. Physically and emotionally he felt terrible, and he had begun to think about possible means of suicide.

During the course of several hours of counseling, I helped him to see the seething anger he had been hiding from himself. There were many, many reasons for it. His mother had died when he was thirteen; his father had died when he was eighteen. He had married at the age of nineteen, but when he was twenty-three, his wife had died of cancer. He had married again, but his second wife was now seriously ill. He had been unjustly accused of dishonesty in his first job and had been forced to resign. Now things were going wrong in his second job too.

Greg had every right to be angry at life, and deep down, though he had concealed it from himself, he was angry with God.

I was able to help him see this, because one of the healing truths of the Christian faith is that God does permit us to express anger against him. In the Old Testament, Moses speaks his mind to the Lord in no uncertain way.

Why have you treated your servant so badly? Why have I not

found favor in your sight, that you lay the burden of all this
people on me? Did I conceive all this people? . . . I am not
able to carry all this people alone, for they are too heavy for
me. If this is the way you are going to treat me, put me to
death at once. . . . and do not let me see my misery. (Num
11:11-15)

The writers of the Psalms are equally forthright:

But I, O LORD, cry out to you;
in the morning my prayer comes before you.
O LORD, why do you cast me off?
Why do you hide your face from me? (Ps 88:13-14)

For I eat ashes like bread,
and mingle tears with my drink,
because of your indignation and anger;
for you have lifted me up and thrown me aside. (Ps 102:9-
10)

Elijah, Job and Jonah all felt free to express their discontent to
God, but the supreme revelation of God's openness to our
anger must be found in the crucifixion. Sinful humankind was
permitted to ram the crown of thorns onto the Son of God and
hammer in the nails. In Archbishop Robert Leighton's remarkable phrase, we are permitted to "vent our rage into the bosom of God."

God the Son died at our hands, but then he rose again, and
amazingly, he still loves us. We could quench his physical life,
but we cannot quench his eternal love.

I was able to share this thought with Greg, and he found the
honesty and courage to express and unleash his anger against

God. Realizing that God still loved him, he was moved to recommit himself to Christ.

Within two weeks Greg was a completely new man. His physical symptoms had disappeared; so had his feelings of depression. He was no longer suicidal. At work he recovered his concentration, and his achievement improved so much that his job was no longer at risk. At home, his wife began to recover; it emerged that her illness had partly been caused by her worries about Greg. So Greg's story had a happy ending.

Not everyone will experience such a quick, spectacular healing, but it is always worthwhile to be honest with God about feelings of anger and depression.

I am privileged to be associated with a group in England called St. Colomba's Fellowship. Its members consist of hospice staff, nurses and others who work among those who are dying. My wife and I are sometimes invited to speak at the fellowship's conferences.

At one of these conferences, we heard a hospice chaplain tell of a patient who asked to see him because he was in great emotional distress. He was in the last stages of cancer and was feeling very guilty because he had spent the previous night ranting, raving and swearing at God. The following morning he felt dreadful. He imagined that his chance of eternal life had now been lost forever, and that God would never forgive one who had so cursed and abused him.

The chaplain asked the patient, "What do you think is the opposite of love?"

The man replied, "Hate."

Very wisely, the chaplain replied, "No, the opposite of love is indifference. You have not been indifferent to God, or you would never have spent the night talking to him, honestly telling him what was in your heart and mind. Do you know the Christian word that describes what you have been doing? The word is 'prayer.' You have spent the night praying."

This insight completely changed the attitude of the hospice patient. Not long after his conversation with the chaplain, he died in peace, trusting the God who remains on speaking terms with us even when our only words for him are words of abuse.

The permission God gives us to be angry with him is one of the supreme and most distinctive Christian privileges. In Islam, disrespect for Allah is unforgivable; it carries the death penalty. Rage against God carries the death penalty in Christianity too, but mysteriously Christ has lovingly borne that penalty on our behalf.

Realizing, then, that God allows us to express our anger against him, how should we pray if we are angry or depressed? We will all find ourselves using different words, but here are some basic principles to guide us.

1. If you are feeling angry at God, it is better by far to admit it than to suppress it. You cannot begin to find healing for yourself if you are unwilling to admit the true nature of your feelings. While God can do something with the honest expression of anger, he can do nothing with bogus piety.

So the first rule is always to be honest with ourselves and honest with God. If your subconscious mind is raging at God, you might as well allow the rage access to your conscious mind also. The miracle of Christian healing is available to you as God ministers to you from the cross of Jesus.

2. In fact, though God is gracious enough to absorb our feelings of anger against himself, often a little thought will show you that these feelings are misplaced. For instance, if you

have been watching televised images of the racked bodies of famine victims, it's important to remember that world hunger is attributable not to God but to human beings. This is a generous planet. If its resources were properly developed and justly distributed, everyone would have enough to live on. The sad fact is that we do not develop or distribute the world's resources in a way that is either fair or intelligent.

The human race is both selfish and stupid, and every time the clock ticks somebody dies to prove it! If that makes us angry, so it should. God is angry too. The proper prayer response is to be penitent for our own part in the world's injustice and to ask God to help us discover what we can do to help those who suffer.

3. There is another type of anger that is considerably less admirable and constructive. Anger can often be totally selfish and misdirected. God forgive us, this is much more common than anger at the injustice of the world.

This kind of anger is rooted in hurt pride, pricked vanity, frustrated selfishness. To cope with it, we need to cultivate a spirit of objectivity. The Scottish poet Robert Burns puts it this way: "O wad some Pow'r the giftie gie us / To see oursels as others see us. / It wad frae mony a blunder free us" (O that some Power would give us the gift to see ourselves as others see us. It would free us from many a blunder).

Then to the spirit of objectivity we need to add a spirit of repentance. As we kneel at the foot of the cross and ask for forgiveness, maybe we can also muster the grace to renounce prejudice and touchiness, and to ask for emotional and spiritual healing. We may not enjoy the process, but we will feel better for it afterward—and so will those around us!

4. There is a fourth type of anger that, though it may look

like the third, is different because it is absolutely justified. This is a sinful, fallen world, and it may very well be that you personally have been unfairly treated. Maybe you have suffered abuse from your parents, your children, your marriage partner, your neighbor or your boss. Maybe a so-called friend has let you down badly, and you feel like the psalmist who said, "Even my bosom friend in whom I trusted . . . has lifted the heel against me" (Ps 41:9).

There is a way to pray for healing under these circumstances too. As always, it will do no good at all to repress your feelings. The rule is to acknowledge your right to anger, but then to give it up voluntarily. We need to learn the healing art of "forgiveness-praying," but for that we will need a whole new chapter.

Heal all that still hurts inside, Lord,

Until I feel whole and strong

Until love and peace abide, Lord,

And forgiveness flows along.

[MARJ DONELLAN]

FOUR

HOW DO YOU PRAY WHEN LIFE HAS HURT YOU?

J esus teaches that when a Christian has been hurt by life, the main weapon we have in our prayer armory is a paradoxical one. It is forgiveness.

Forgiveness has the power to free us from the harm our grudges can bring upon us. It can also sometimes have the power to turn our enemies into our friends. Learning the art of "forgiveness-praying" can transform life in a spectacular way.

Many years ago, I was grateful to come across an excellent method of forgiveness-praying. It was typed on a sheet of paper, without any indication of its source or its author. I am taking the liberty of reproducing it now, with grateful acknowledgments to its anonymous originator.

Like the method of testing oneself by the Ten Commandments, which we considered in chapter two, this prayer sequence is remarkably potent. If it does not get you sooner, it gets you later because it covers so many of life's significant areas. Not all of it will apply to you, but you will feel your inner self reverberate whenever a sensitive area is touched. If you let the Holy Spirit move freely in you, your mind will be guided to the persons or groups whom you personally need to forgive, even if they are not specifically named.

Here is the prayer. Take a deep breath, and, in the name of the Father and of the Son and of the Holy Spirit—have a go.

Lord Jesus Christ, I ask today for your help that I may forgive everyone in my life who has hurt me. I know that you will give me strength to forgive, and I thank you that you love me more than I love myself and want my happiness more than I desire it for myself.

Lord, I truly forgive MYSELF for my sins, faults and failings. For all that is truly bad in myself or all that I think is bad, I do forgive myself.

For any delvings in the occult, horoscopes, séances, fortune-telling.

For taking your Name in vain. For not worshiping you.

For hurting my parents; for getting drunk, for taking dope. For sins against my purity, for adultery, for abortion, for stealing, for lying, I am truly forgiving myself today. Thank you, Lord, for your grace in this moment.

I truly forgive my MOTHER. I forgive her for all the times she hurt or resented me, for being angry with me and for all the times she punished me. I forgive her for the times she preferred my brothers and sisters to me. I forgive her for the times she called me dumb, ugly, stupid, the worst of the children, and for saying that I cost the family a lot of money. For the times she told me I was unwanted, an accident, a mistake, or not what she expected, I forgive her.

I forgive my FATHER. I forgive him for any nonsupport, lack of love, affection or attention. I forgive him for any lack of time, for not giving me his companionship, for his drinking, arguing and fighting with my mother or the other children. For his severe punishments, for desertion, for being away from home, for divorcing my mother or for any running around, I do forgive him.

Lord, I extend my forgiveness to my SISTERS and BROTHERS. I forgive those who rejected me, lied about me, hated me, resented me, competed for my parents' love. Those who hurt me or physically harmed me, those who were too severe on me, punished me or made my life unpleasant in any way—I do forgive them.

Lord, I forgive my SPOUSE for lack of love, affection, consideration, attention, support, communication, for faults, failings, weaknesses and those other acts or words that hurt or disturb me.

Jesus, I forgive my CHILDREN for their lack of respect, obedience, love, attention, support, warmth, understanding. For their bad habits, falling away from the church, any actions which disturb me, I forgive them.

My God, I forgive my SON/DAUGHTER-IN-LAW and other relatives by marriage, who treat my child with a lack of love. For all their words, thoughts, actions or omissions which injure and cause pain, I forgive them.

Please help me to forgive my RELATIVES, my grandmother and grandfather, who may have interfered in our family, been possessive of my parents, caused confusion or turned one parent against another.

Jesus, help me to forgive my COWORKERS who are disagreeable or who make life miserable for me. . . . For those who push their work off on to me, gossip about me, won't cooperate, try to take my job, I do forgive them.

My NEIGHBORS need to be forgiven, Lord, for all their noise, for letting their property run down, for not tying up the dog, for not taking in the garbage bins, for running down the neighborhood. I do forgive them.

I now forgive my PASTOR, my CONGREGATION and my CHURCH for all their lack of support, pettiness, lack of friendliness; for not affirming me as they should, not providing me with inspiration, for not using me in a key position, for not inviting me to serve in a major capacity and for any other hurt they have inflicted, I do forgive them today.

Lord, I forgive my EMPLOYER for not paying me enough money, for not appreciating my work, for being unkind and unreasonable with me, for being angry or unfriendly, for not promoting me and for not complimenting me on my work.

Lord, I forgive my SCHOOLTEACHERS and INSTRUCTORS of the past as well as the present. I forgive those who punished me, humiliated me, insulted me, treated me unjustly, made fun of me, called me dumb or stupid, made me stay after school.

Lord, I forgive my FRIENDS who have let me down, lost contact with me, do not support me, were not available when I needed help, borrowed money and did not return it, gossiped about me.

Lord Jesus, I especially pray for the grace of forgiveness for that ONE PERSON who has hurt me most. I ask to forgive anyone whom I consider my greatest enemy, the one who is the hardest to forgive or the one whom I said I would never forgive.

Thank you, Jesus, that your will is to free me from the evil of unforgiveness. Let that will be done.

Let your Holy Spirit fill me with light, and let every dark area of my mind be enlightened. Amen.

A number of elements in this prayer are well worth further examination.

The self-forgiveness section at the start is essential. We often forget it, but if we fail to forgive ourselves, we won't find it easy to forgive anyone else. We will tend to be prickly and ungracious people, spending so much time and energy on internal turmoil that our freedom for effective Christian living will be seriously impaired.

Of course, all that was said in chapter two about how to pray if we feel guilty or ashamed remains true. We need to admit the facts, say we are sorry and go to the foot of the cross to ask for forgiveness. But then it is vital for our health of spirit that we not only acknowledge with gratitude that God has forgiven us but also follow God's lead. If God has forgiven us, it's really rather presumptuous for us to fail to forgive ourselves.

The results can be remarkable. Some years ago we invited a young South African evangelist to visit our church. He had a glorious singing voice and used it most effectively in presenting the gospel, using an excellent tape player with a variety of superb musical accompaniments.

But on the Sunday morning when he visited us, he got off to a terrible start. Perhaps he had put in the wrong tape or pressed the wrong button; at any rate, he found himself singing quite the wrong song. It had nothing to do with his introduction, and we all felt distinctly embarrassed for him. We were afraid that his whole presentation might be spoiled—but that was far from the case. He sorted out the electronics, and his second song was fine. His third was better still. His spoken words were everything that could have been desired.

I asked him afterward how he had managed to make such a superb recovery. His reply was, "When things go wrong I have learned the art of instant self-forgiveness."

Of course, he was absolutely right. Just because you have made a mess of part of your day, there is no need to make yourself so miserable that you automatically mess up the rest of it as well! Self-forgiveness is an essential tool for effective living.

After the section on self-forgiveness, the prayer quoted above encourages us to forgive our parents for any ill that they have done us, or that we imagine they have done us. This is an important element in healing prayer, even if our parents are long dead, because the act of forgiveness is as much for our own sake as for theirs.

Standard techniques for "healing the memories" can be part of this prayer—picturing a hurtful situation from the past but inviting Jesus to be present with us in the memory. As we allow him to influence our feelings and reactions, he will lead us to new understanding and a new capacity for forgiveness.

Perhaps the most important phrase in the prayer comes just before the end. "Thank you, Jesus, that your will is to free me from the evil of unforgiveness."

Unforgiveness is an evil at many levels. Clearly it hurts us emotionally, because it can bind and obsess our thought processes in all kinds of ways. It also hurts us physically. Learning the art of forgiveness-praying can sometimes produce a physical healing that seems little short of miraculous.

Martha was eaten up with arthritis. She was largely confined to a wheelchair and was in continuous pain. One day, she had herself pushed to a Christian healing center, where she asked for a laying on of hands. Those who prayed with her proceeded to teach her a method of forgiveness-praying not unlike the one in this chapter. She was advised to forgive someone every day until she ran out of people to forgive, and to follow up each prayer of forgiveness with a practical act to show that her forgiveness was real—writing a letter, making a phone call, offering a gift, trying to restore a broken relationship.

Six weeks later she returned to the healing center, and no-body recognized her because this time she *walked* in, totally free of arthritis and looking twenty years younger!

If the emotional and physical results of forgiveness-praying can be spectacular, its spiritual results are even greater. Jesus tells us that if we have a spirit of unforgiveness, it can obstruct our union with Christ and block our salvation. This is the message of the parable of the unforgiving servant in Matthew 18:21-35.

There is no receiving of forgiveness without a corresponding willingness to forgive. Forgiving and being forgiven are two sides of the same coin. No wonder the Lord's Prayer contains the words, "Forgive us our debts, as we also have forgiven our debtors." Forgiveness-praying is a necessary ingredient in our preparation for eternal life.

So: "Thank you, Jesus, that your will is to free me from the evil of unforgiveness." I cannot manage it in my own strength, but mercifully I do not have to do so. It is because Jesus lovingly forgives me that I can allow his loving forgiveness to spill over out of my life into the world around me!

One final thought before this chapter ends. Forgiving is not forgetting. It is remembering—but going on loving just the same. It is not a blurring of the distinction between right and wrong. It is not ceasing to fight against evil. It is not pretending that you are not angry when you are. It is seeing things exactly as they are, but keeping a loving relationship open by the power of Christ, who keeps a loving relationship open with us in spite of the pain we cause him.

George Sinker used to tell the story of a dream he had while he was serving in India as Bishop of Nagpur. On a hot day he fell asleep in his garden and dreamed he was wandering about the garden looking for a cup so that he could fetch water to quench his thirst. At the end of the garden, he found a table covered in cups. Some were large. Some were small. One was absolutely tiny.

He was just about to pick the largest one, when the tiniest one spoke to him in a little tinkling voice. "Choose me," it said. "I don't hold much, but I overflow lots." He woke up and recognized this as a symbol of Christian living.

We Christians may not hold much, but by the grace of God we can overflow. Jesus said, "Love one another as I have loved you" (Jn 15:12). His love is our resource. Our love is a response to his love. His forgiveness is our resource. Our forgiveness is a response to his forgiveness.

So by his grace and saving power, when life has hurt us we can respond with forgiveness. Forgiveness-praying can change your life. It can be a path to healing. "Thank you, Jesus, that your will is to free me from the evil of unforgiveness. Let that will be done."

Perfect love

casts out fear.

[1 JOHN 4:18]

God loves you as though you were

the only person in

the world.

[ST. AUGUSTINE]

FIVE

HOW DO YOU PRAY WHEN YOU ARE ANXIOUS OR FEARFUL?

*I*n the last two chapters, we have seen that anger can be a major hazard in life. Whether we express it without restraint or bottle it up in our subconscious mind, it can do all sorts of damage.

In this chapter, we come to a greater danger still: a hazard that threatens health, wholeness and even the survival of the human race. It is fear.

The Bible recognizes how common the spirit of fear is and how deadly it can be. On seventy-nine different occasions the

Scriptures record the command "Fear not."

Fear influences human behavior in many ways, and it's probably no exaggeration to say that it is at the root of most human problems.

Sometimes it shows itself in a relatively straightforward fashion. People who suffer from undisguised fearfulness both feel anxious and look anxious. Even if they have nothing in particular to worry about, they will invent something. The root of fearfulness is within them. They know it and they show it.

We may feel very sorry for such folk, but actually, they are among the more fortunate of the fearful. What they honestly feel they honestly admit. Because they acknowledge their problem in a straightforward way, they have already taken the first steps along the road that can lead to healing.

Because fearfulness is so painful, it is more usual to try to hide behind one or another of a series of well-tried defense mechanisms. For instance, I may take the view that though I feel insecure myself, other people seem much more self-assured. I may therefore imagine that if only I can attract the attention of others, some of their security will rub off on me, and I will feel better. If I choose this sort of defense pattern against fear and anxiety, I will become an attention-seeker, a manipulator.

I may look confident. I may be the life and soul of the party. Less-discerning onlookers may envy my apparent lack of fearfulness, but inwardly I will be in a state of panic, and my relationships will not be open and trusting. I will be prevented from doing anything about it by the fact that I am trying to keep both my fearfulness and my defense mechanism well out of my conscious mind.

Or I may take the view that there is no security in others,

that other people are frightening. I may agree with Jean-Paul Sartre that "hell is the other person." In that case, I must keep others away. I must build some kind of wall of detachment and hide behind it.

I may become a successful professional and hide behind my professionalism—a doctor hiding behind the white coat, a pastor hiding behind a clerical collar, an actor hiding behind a role, an intellectual hiding behind a wall of books. I may look so successful and secure that the world will envy me, but inwardly, hidden from the world and perhaps from myself, I will be a very different person. The world will be very surprised when I have an emotional breakdown!

Or I may employ another defense mechanism and take uncertain refuge in a phobia. This is a mental trick, well fancied by many a subconscious mind. I tell myself that most of life is perfectly safe, and I restrict my fearfulness to one symbolic thing. It may be a fear of dogs, or snakes, or heights, or crowds, or open spaces or closed spaces. It may be almost anything. I tell myself that this symbolic thing is terrifying, but otherwise life is fine.

Unfortunately, this is a defense mechanism of diminishing returns. The phobia can start to grow until it becomes almost all-pervading. For instance, the person afraid of open spaces can come to the point that only home is safe, and then perhaps only one room in the home.

Some prefer to retreat into fantasy. Our minds have extraordinary inventive powers. We can build up an interior world in which we are powerful and adulated, perhaps sexually irresistible, perhaps possessing magic endowments, able to take revenge on any who displease us—but then, of course, we have to come out into the real world, and the fantasy is exposed for the unreal thing it is. The real world is as bad as ever, or even worse. This may be so intolerable that the two worlds begin to impinge. This way lies madness, the beginning of psychopathic violence.

Some go straight to violence. They think, "I can't have time to feel insecure if I'm beating others up." But an aggressive exterior can conceal an interior of quivering jelly! This defense is sometimes used not just by individuals but even by a whole nation.

Still others seek refuge in a security symbol, such as money, fame, glamour, power, prestige or popularity. We treat these things almost as though they were gods, able to deliver from the fear within—but whether we attain them or not, they fail us again and again. Like the defense mechanism of aggression, this one can be used at a national level.

The world is full of individuals and collective groups who are trapped, enmeshed and virtually enslaved by their own defense mechanisms. Mental tricks that were designed to affirm and free us from fearfulness end up doing the precise opposite. It makes sense to resist them. They do not work, and, to make matters worse, they sometimes bring physical problems with them—digestive problems, perhaps, or skin conditions.

Maybe this has been a painful chapter so far. Maybe somewhere along the line you have recognized yourself—as I have to admit I have.

If so, congratulations! You have taken the first step toward the healing of anxiety and fear. There is a gospel procedure to deal with fear. Jesus wouldn't say "Fear not" to us unless he could offer resources that could lead us into deliverance from fear.

The first step is to admit our insecurities. We can then go to our Lord and avail ourselves of his healing resources.

So what does Jesus say to us as we go to him in fear and trembling? He first assures us that he really does understand fear and anxiety. He understands these feelings not just in a theoretical way but from his own experience. He knows them from the inside.

Remember those strange words from the cross, "Eloi, Eloi, lama sabachthani"—"My God, my God, why have you forsaken me?" Here is a strange miracle: God the Son is allowed to experience what it is like to feel God-forsaken. This is the spirit of fearfulness in its deepest form. This is total dereliction.

So Jesus meets us in our place of anxiety and fearfulness. However low we may fall, he has plumbed yet greater depths. As the psalmist says, "If I make my bed in Sheol [the world of the dead], you are there" (Ps 139:8). Jesus meets us at our darkest time in our darkest place, and he holds us to himself.

He assures us that we have been made by God the Father, and that God does not make rubbish. He assures us that we are loved by God and that God's perfect love has the power to cast out all fear. He assures us that we are wanted by God. God has something for us to do and to be in his service. Without our involvement, part of God's purpose will be eternally unfulfilled, because each one of us is precious and unique.

How then do you pray when you are anxious or fearful? You just meet Jesus and allow him to surround you with his own special love—and the power of that love cannot be overestimated.

Meryl was emotionally ill. She had been so for years. She had been seen by several consultants, but there had been no cure;

in fact, she was regarded as incurable. She felt there was no hope, no future for her. All she could feel was fearfulness, pointlessness, despair.

When she was at her lowest, a Christian friend came around with a sheet of paper. She had been searching her Bible and had found twenty-two texts, all about the love of God. She said, "Will you read these every day, morning and evening, very slowly and prayerfully, letting them soak into you, for as long as it takes till they begin to make a difference?"

Meryl agreed to do so, and gradually but unmistakably something started to happen. A slow-motion miracle began to take place. In six months, Meryl was absolutely healed.

I know this is true because Meryl told me the story herself and showed me her well-worn piece of paper containing the twenty-two texts. She could hardly find words to describe the difference they had made to her. Through her, they were now making a difference to others too, because another fact you should know about Meryl is that she is a doctor by profession. Her illness had made it impossible for her to work, but once she received the healing power of Jesus, she was set free to serve her patients once again.

Dr. Meryl has told me I may share these twenty-two verses with anyone who might be helped by them. So here they are for you to savor for your own healing and delight, and for you to copy out and give to others who may need them. God bless you, and others through you, as you use them.

Do not fear, for I have redeemed you (Is 43:1). I am with you (Is 43:5). And remember, I am with you always, to the end of the age (Mt 28:20).

Do not let your hearts be troubled. Believe in God, believe also in me (Jn 14:1). I will help you (Is 41:14). When you pass through the waters, I will be with you; and through the rivers, they shall not overwhelm you; when you walk through fire you shall not be burned (Is 43:2).

Do not be afraid (Lk 12:7). Even the hairs of your head are all counted. So do not be afraid (Mt 10:30). The mountains may depart and the hills be removed, but my steadfast love shall not depart from you, and my covenant of peace shall not be removed (Is 54:10).

Come, my beloved (Song 7:11). I will take you . . . in righteousness and in justice, in steadfast love, and in mercy. I will take you . . . in faithfulness, and you shall know the LORD (Hos 2:19-20). I AM WHO I AM (Ex 3:14). I am the LORD your God (Ex 20:2).

As the Father has loved me, so I have loved you (Jn 15:9). I have called you by name, you are mine (Is 43:1). Before I formed you in the womb I knew you, and before you were born I consecrated you (Jer 1:5). You did not choose me but I chose you (Jn 15:16).

You are precious in my sight, and honored, and I love you (Is 43:4). I have loved you with an everlasting love; therefore I have continued my faithfulness to you (Jer 31:3). How can I give you up? . . . My compassion grows warm and tender (Hos 11:8).

Can a woman forget her nursing child, or show no compassion for the child of her womb? Even these may forget, yet I will not forget you. See I have inscribed you in the palms of my hands (Is 49:15-16). For I, the LORD your God, hold you by the right hand (Is 41:13).

As Meryl's story illustrates, God's healing plan for the fearful begins as he fills us with his love. He takes the initiative. Through Jesus Christ, he comes where we are, meets us in our place of need and loves us totally, whatever the cost of the love to Himself.

This is the love that heals anxiety. This is the love that casts out fear. It may take a long time. It may even take a lifetime. But, as Paul says, nothing can separate us from God's love (Rom 8:38). If we are willing to be loved, God is willing to love us, and to go on and on loving until love's healing work is done.

Then, as Meryl's story also shows, God's "fill and spill" policy begins to work. We find ourselves motivated and liberated to love others. "We love because he first loved us" (1 Jn 4:19). We become links in God's chain reaction of love. We receive healing so that we ourselves can bring healing to others.

Drop thy still dews of quietness

Till all our strivings cease;

Take from our souls the strain and stress,

And let our ordered lives confess

The beauty of thy peace.

[JOHN GREENLEAF WHITTIER]

SIX

HOW DO YOU PRAY WHEN YOU ARE BUSY AND STRESSED?

Y ou may well have experienced feelings of relief as you read the title of this chapter. Guilt, shame, anger, depression and fear are all deeply traumatic emotions. Busyness seems a mercifully lightweight problem by comparison.

In fact, being busy is in many ways a blessing. I remember that as a small boy I used to envy busy people. I was an only child, and I often felt rather lonely. People who had full lives seemed to me to be very fortunate. I used to dread the thought of having nothing to do.

But I've now learned that you can have too much of a good thing. You can be so busy that life becomes pressured and stressful. Even the best-ordered lives will have times when there is just too much to do for the time available.

How should we pray during such times? Here are five suggestions.

First, it should always be a Christian goal to begin the day with God in a way that is disciplined and preplanned. An unhurried time of prayer at the outset of the day is a deeply enriching investment. It establishes our sense of direction and clarifies our aims and actually *saves* time in the long run.

If, for one reason or another, it is completely impracticable to find time for prayer at the beginning of some days, then follow this golden rule: Offer the first free time of the day to God, however and whenever it comes. This wouldn't be the best way to manage all of one's life, but it's certainly a great deal better than forgetting prayer altogether.

Secondly, learn the art of the "arrow-prayer"—just a few words of prayer shot like an arrow into the heart of any situation of need, whenever it occurs.

Some of the most famous prayers are short ones. It has been so through the centuries. Here are a few from the Bible in their traditional form:

Speak, Lord, for thy servant heareth. (The prophet Samuel in the early eleventh century B.C.)

I will lay me down in peace and take my rest, for it is thou, Lord, that makest me dwell in safety. (King David in the late eleventh century B.C.)

Here I am, send me. (The prophet Isaiah in the mid-eighth century B.C.)

Amen. Even so come, Lord Jesus. (The apostle John in the first century A.D.)

And a few more from other sources:

May God of his goodness and love keep me. (King Canute,

who reigned in England from 1016 to 1035)

O God, of Thy goodness, give me Thyself, for only in Thee have I all. (Julian of Norwich, 1343)

O Saviour of the world, who by Thy Cross and precious blood hast redeemed us, save us and help us, we humbly beseech Thee, O Lord. (1549 *Book of Common Prayer*)

O Lord, Thou knowest how busy we must be this day; if we forget Thee, do not Thou forget us. (General Lord Astley before the Battle of Edgehill, 1642)

And last, but not least, from the founder of Methodism:

Lord, let us not live to be useless. (John Wesley, 1703)

Jesus himself used arrow prayers, such as "Not what I want but what you want" (Mt 26:39) and "Father, into your hands I commend my spirit" (Lk 23:46). We can use his prayers for ourselves. We can also use any of the other biblical or nonbiblical prayers that are appropriate.

In the stress of a busy moment, though, we will find that we make up our own arrow prayers, and they may be very simple indeed—"Lord help me," or even the single word "Jesus." Then, when we are coping again, a quick "Thank you, Lord" does not come amiss.

It is a mark of grace if we do not confine our arrow prayers to our own needs, but if we adopt the practice of instant prayer on behalf of others, lifting them before God at the moment when we realize their need. All too often we think, "I must pray about this later," when we could be using the same seconds to pray "Lord, help John to cope," "Lord, heal and support Mary."

Third, when we are busy and stressed, it's important to learn about the spiritual art that Brother Lawrence called "the practice of the presence of God." God is not only with us when we turn aside from the work pressures of the day and find a quiet time and place to say our prayers. He is also with us in the activity and bustle of our busiest moments. Practicing the presence of God means converting this knowledge from a piece of theoretical theology into an actual personal experience.

To do this effectively, we need to take the psychological process of association as a prayer asset. There are scenes, experiences and objects that you automatically associate with this or that person. For instance, the smell of newly baked white bread takes me back to my grandmother's kitchen, where she and my aunts used to bake for the family. A television series set on the campus of Oxford University takes me back to my student days there, and I find myself picturing the faces of old friends.

Practicing the presence of God involves using the process of association continually to remind ourselves of the Lord. For instance, on my desk I have some beautifully marked stones that I have collected from different beaches. Not only do they serve as paperweights, but they also remind me of the creative power of God. They are aids to the practice of his presence. Others might consider it odd, but it works for me. Different things remind different people of God's presence.

Bishop George Sinker, whose dream in an Indian garden I mentioned in an earlier chapter, developed the habit of associating doors with the presence of God. Every time he went through a door he would silently say, "Lord, come with me through this door." It is not surprising that he often brought a sense of God's presence with him when he entered a room.

You can evolve your own procedures as you practice the presence of God. If you have a watch that beeps every hour, you could adopt the habit of saying silently, "Lord, this hour comes from you. I give it back to you." You can offer life's waiting time to God. For instance, when you are making a telephone call, the ten, twenty or thirty seconds during which you wait, holding the receiver as you listen to the ringing tone, can become a time for practicing the presence of the God who so often waits for us to respond to him. The same is true of the time you spend in your car, waiting for a red traffic light to change to green. It can be a praying time rather than a fuming time. And do the same thing when you get caught in a traffic jam. You can have your mind on the Lord rather than your fingers on the car horn!

Clearly, there is double benefit in this. Fussing, fretting and fuming are harmful to the body, mind and spirit. Practicing the presence of God turns a time of waiting into a bonus.

There are no limits to this prayer method. It requires no extra time whatsoever. It is very much a do-it-yourself procedure. Everyone can work out his or her own system.

The poet and hymn-writer George Herbert put it in a nutshell when he wrote:

Teach me, my God and King
In all things Thee to see;
And what I do in anything
To do it as for Thee.

This is a prayer-principle that can transform the humdrum into something special—or, as Herbert put it, can "make drudgery divine."

A kitchen sink can almost turn into a little altar, when pots and pans and water taps are used as prayer reminders. Any errand you have to go on can become a "walk with God." You can walk on a particular side of the sidewalk as a reminder that

God is with you. Even the act of breathing can be a powerful reminder that we are invited to take in all the goodness of God's Spirit, and let out the sins and lies that spoil life.

Fourth, beware of the heresy of supposing that we have to give God "the works" in prayer before it will do any good, that time and tears and earnest persuasion are required to wrest an answer from his reluctant hand. God is not like that, and prayer is not like that. God is good, and the basic prayer mode is just resting in his goodness. God wants the best for us and for all creation. The essence of prayer is simply affirming God's will, rejoicing in God's will, relaxing into God's will. Knowing this can bring a still center into the maelstrom of a busy day.

Suppose you have five minutes available before the next job must be done. How can you turn it into a little oasis of stillness and re-creation?

You will need to put your body at ease. So sit in a comfortable chair with your feet flat on the floor (or on a footrest, if one is available) and your hands on your knees. Your head should be supported, or if the chair you are using does not have a headrest, you can allow your head to fall forward a little. Breathe steadily and deeply. My wife, who is a physical therapist, tells me that if you concentrate on breathing out, the breathing in will take care of itself.

Clear your mind of extraneous thoughts, and then recollect one of the biblical texts that lead to stillness. "Be still, and know that I am God" (Ps 46:10). "In quietness and in trust shall be your strength" (Is 30:15). "Come to me, all you that are weary and are carrying heavy burdens, and I will give you rest" (Mt 11:28). "Peace I leave with you; my peace I give to you" (Jn 14:27).

Enjoy the peace of God. If you find it helpful, use a small

part of the "ring of peace" method of prayer, which we will consider in chapter eight. Let God do the work.

St. Anselm puts in beautifully: "Come now . . . flee for a while from your tasks, hide yourself for a little space from the turmoil of your thoughts. Come, cast aside your burdensome cares, put aside your laborious pursuits for a little while, give your time to God and rest in him for a little while." Even five minutes of God-centered stillness can make a difference to the course of a busy day.

So far I've made suggestions about how to pray when we are busy and stressed without changing the structures of our life, or using time that was earmarked for other things. Yet it's possible that we'll find that our prayers do not leave our work schedule unscathed. Part of God's purpose through our prayers may be to show us that we are structuring our lives wrongly. So if you are feeling busy and stressed because of your lifestyle, my fifth suggestion is that at some point it's important to offer that pattern of life to God and ask whether he wants you to change your priorities. Just as we cannot ask God to bless a wrong deed, so we cannot ask him to bless a wrong life-pattern.

Many years ago I learned this the hard way. In my early days at university, I made sure that though I worked fairly hard from Monday to Saturday, Sunday was different. That was a day for worship and recreation, as the Bible says it should be.

As the months went by, my first set of exams drew near, and Sunday began to blur into all the other days. In the interest of a good exam result, I decided that though I would worship each Sunday, I would also work on Sundays. It was a mistake— as it always is to disobey God's commands.

For a brief period my work rate went up, but after a few weeks, I was surprised to find that I was actually doing less work in seven days than I had previously done in six. The day of rest was not only a biblical command for the good of my soul. It was a common-sense prescription for the health of my mind and my body. A life in which each day is a replica of every other day and no day is special erases the rhythms and variations of life that are necessary for our physical and psychological wholeness.

"Remember the sabbath day, and keep it holy. Six days you shall labor and do all your work. But the seventh day is a sabbath to the LORD your God" (Ex 20:8-10). I had to hear these words again and correct my pattern of life. Almost immediately my work rate went up again—and, in due course, the exams took care of themselves.

So how do you pray when you are busy and stressed? Make sure that amid the busyness you search for the minutes and moments in which to reach out to God. Start the day with him, and keep renewing your contact through the prayer techniques contained in the earlier part of this chapter. If this does not solve the problem, it will be necessary to ask God's help to check the overall structures and patterns of your life to see if there is lack of balance, or a lack of obedience to God's law.

Some very basic rules of life have been helpful to me over the years whenever workaholism has reared its hungry head and I've needed to review my life's priorities. You may be familiar with these sayings already, but perhaps you'll benefit from the reminder, as I do.

1. Seven prayerless days make one weak.

2. If I am too busy for God, then I am *too busy*.

3. People are more important than things.

4. All work and no play makes Roy a dull boy.

5. Nobody is indispensable but God!

The world will be at the feet of those who are themselves at the feet of Jesus Christ—that is the surest thing I know.

[DICK SHEPPARD]

SEVEN

HOW DO YOU PRAY WHEN YOU FEEL JEALOUS OR ENVIOUS?

---

*J*ealousy is a common state of mind. Most of us fall into it from time to time, and sometimes we even cherish it as though it were a precious and desirable attitude to have. Yet the truth is precisely the opposite.

Jealousy is bad for us from virtually every point of view. It damages us emotionally, spiritually and physically. If we allow ourselves to be impaled upon its hooks, it makes us nasty, miserable and ill.

There is a good illustration of this in 1 Kings 21. This chapter tells the story of King Ahab, who was a rich and powerful man. Materially speaking, he had almost everything a man could desire. However, there was something that spoiled his sense of well-being. Close to his palace, there was a vineyard that he did not own. The king wanted this piece of land to plant as a vegetable garden, but its owner, Naboth, would not sell it, because his family had owned it for a long time.

The more Ahab thought about it, the more covetous and jealous he felt, and the more obsessed he became with his desire to possess Naboth's vineyard. He fumed, he fretted, he lapsed into an angry depression. His jealousy and envy took away his energy, his appetite and his peace of mind. And though he ultimately acquired the vineyard with the unprincipled help of his wife, the murderous Queen Jezebel, his state of mind was severely impaired afterward.

Jealousy was not the path to happiness for Ahab. It never is for any one of us.

For a more down-to-earth, contemporary illustration, I find myself thinking of a young woman who once talked to me about her jealousy problem. She loved televised game shows, yet she never watched them. The trouble was that she was hooked on the sin of jealousy, and every time a contestant won a prize, she felt so envious that she had to turn the television off. It's no fun being jealous.

One of the reasons jealousy impairs our health and happiness is that it is incompatible with love. "Love is not envious," says the apostle Paul (1 Cor 13:14). If we do not allow love to drive out jealousy, then jealousy will drive out love, and life without love is not worth living.

Another reason to deal with jealous feelings rather than harboring them is that they are often signs that we are not valuing ourselves as we should. True Christian self-respect is not dependent on external factors. Those who have true respect for themselves can stand with head held high even in the most adverse circumstances.

When Paul was brought as a prisoner in chains before King Agrippa and Governor Festus, they must have been an impressive sight, bedecked, as they were, in all the trappings of royal splendor and military pomp. In his pain and humiliation, Paul could well have envied them. But, on the contrary, in spite of the discomfort of his chains, he was aware of the spiritual status he enjoyed as a Christian. Far from envying Agrippa and Festus, he longed to share his spiritual riches with them. "I pray to God," he said, "that not only you but also all who are listening to me today might become such as I am—except for these chains" (Acts 26:29).

The German pastor Dietrich Bonhoeffer was subjected to terrible ordeals in Nazi prisons during World War II. Other prisoners howled and beat with their fists against the locked doors of their cells, particularly during the heavy bombing of Berlin. But Bonhoeffer, though he admitted he felt weak and vulnerable, amazed everybody with his attitude of quiet calm. Like Paul, he held his head high.

He wrote, "They often tell me I stepped from my cell's confinement calmly, cheerfully, firmly like a squire from his country house. They often tell me I used to speak to my warders freely and friendlily and clearly, as though it were mine to command." He seemed to covet nothing but the opportunity to minister to those who were in prison with him.

An even more basic reason to avoid jealousy is that not only is it incompatible with Christian love and self-respect, but it also betrays a wrong attitude to God himself. Paul goes as far as to say that "greed . . . is idolatry" (Col 3:5). For the jealous person, material possessions and earthly glory are more important than God's Law, which clearly states, "You shall not covet" (Ex 20:17).

So if jealousy is such an undesirable thing, what are the prayer principles by which we can correct it?

1. It's important to see the damaging nature of jealousy very clearly, and to know that its effects are totally undesirable. It's also important to reject and renounce the sin of jealousy very specifically before God, and to ask his help in rooting it out of your life.

If, having done this, you find you are still struggling against the temptation to be jealous, then as soon as the temptation enters your mind, you may find it can be driven out by saying quite sharply to yourself, "In the name of God, *stop it!*"

2. Affirm before God that love is "a still more excellent way" (1 Cor 12:31). Since love is a fruit of the Holy Spirit (Gal 5:22), open yourself anew to the Holy Spirit, and ask that love may grow in you and nudge aside all inclination to jealousy or envy. It may be helpful to use the meditation on the healing work of the Holy Spirit in chapter eight as a means of doing this.

3. Affirm your own value as a human being. This value has nothing to do with possessions or popularity or power or prestige, or any of the perquisites we are tempted to covet.

Many years ago, I learned that my personal value does not rest on any achievement of my own, but on the three basic truths about God that I mentioned in chapter five: (1) God made me and offers himself as my Father; therefore, despising myself would be an insult to his creatorship and fatherhood. (2) God loves me with an amazing sacrificial love that did not even stop short of offering his Son to die for me upon the cross; therefore, for me to despise myself would be an insult to the redemptive love of Jesus. (3) God wants me and calls me by the Holy Spirit to his service; so for me to despise myself would be an insult to the Holy Spirit.

It is because of the nature of God that we can, and should, affirm ourselves, and I believe it is a wholesome spiritual exercise to say several times each day, slowly and deliberately, "God made me. God loves me. God wants me." Envy of other people becomes irrelevant when we realize that if we are treasured by God, then we need no social position or perquisites to bolster our sense of value.

4. Above all, we correct our wrong perspective as we respond to all that God has done for us with love and worship and longing. Joy Davidman has put this thought supremely well in her book *Smoke on the Mountain.* She says, "There is, in the last analysis, only one way to stop covetousness and the destruction of body and soul that spring from covetousness, and that is to want God so much that we can't be bothered with inordinate wants for anything else."

God wills healing of

the body and mind.

[JAMIE BUCKINGHAM]

EIGHT

HOW DO YOU PRAY WHEN YOU OR OTHERS ARE ILL?

A mistake we often make about healing prayer is to suppose that if it is to be effective, it must necessarily involve great effort. We think of it as hard work, as striving, almost as wrestling with God, like Jacob's wrestling with the angel at Peniel in Genesis 32.

This is the way I myself used to think. In fact, often after praying for somebody's healing, I would find the imprints of my own nails on my palms because I had been clenching my fists so tightly as I agonized in prayer.

But I am now certain that usually prayer has more to do with resting than with striving, and that this is particularly so when we, or those we love, are in trouble. In Matthew 11:28, Jesus said, "Come to me, all you that are weary and are carrying heavy burdens, and I will give you"—what? A heavier pack to carry? A bigger workload? No. In the first instance, the promise of Jesus to those who are weary and burdened is "I will give you rest"—or, in another translation, "I will refresh you."

We tend not to understand the primacy of rest in prayer. In fact, we tend not to understand the primacy of rest in the whole of Christian living. There is a lovely piece of music by Mendelssohn called "O Rest in the Lord," but in church circles we generally play it only at funerals!

For a true biblical perspective on Christian prayer and Christian achievement, we need to study John 15:1-8, the lovely picture of the vine and the branches. Jesus says that he is the vine, God the Father is the gardener, and we, his followers, are the branches. How does the branch bear fruit? By striving? Agonizing? Throwing itself into a frenzy of activity? No. The fruit comes simply because the branch "abides" in the vine.

Through this picture, Jesus is saying to us, Calm down, rest in me, let me do the work and provide the resources, and then the fruit will take care of itself. "Abide in me as I abide in you. Just as the branch cannot bear fruit by itself unless it abides in the vine, neither can you unless you abide in me. I am the vine, you are the branches. Those who abide in me and I in them bear much fruit, because apart from me you can do nothing" (Jn 15:4-5).

If we want to live lives that are fruitful, we must learn to "abide." If we want to pray prayers that are fruitful, we must learn to "abide."

This principle holds for human relationships. The best relationships (a really good marriage, for instance) are produced when people feel able to "abide" in each other. It is also true of our relationship with God. Through Jesus, we are privileged to abide in God and to have God abiding in us.

This is the basic principle of the three healing prayer methods that constitute the rest of this chapter. The first is a means of resting in the healing peace of God the Father. The second is a means of resting in the healing presence of God the Son. The third is a means of resting in the healing power of God the Holy Spirit. All three methods were first published in my earlier book *Christian Healing Rediscovered* (pages 38, 87 and 108 in the InterVarsity Press edition), but now I want to offer a rather fuller version.

My suggestion is that you read the rest of this chapter slowly and prayerfully. After you finish reading about each method of prayer, put the book down and spend at least ten minutes practicing the prayer method and making it your own.

The Ring of Peace

I call the first method "the ring of peace." For the sake of convenience, I've divided it into numbered steps.

1. Begin by recollecting the presence of Christ. If you are praying within a group, your group has the promise of Jesus—"Where two or three are gathered in my name, I am there among them" (Mt 18:20). If you are in private prayer, he is still with you. You have his word—"I am with you always, to the end of the age" (Mt 28:20). It is good to remember the simple, old-fashioned comment of the Scottish missionary David Livingstone on this text: "This is the word of a gentleman of the most sacred and strictest honor, and there's an end on't!"

2. So there you are, you and Jesus. What sort of experience is it to be in his presence? He has not changed. He is "the same yesterday and today and forever" (Heb 13:8). He is the same Jesus who went about preaching the gospel of the kingdom and healing all kinds of sickness and disease among the people (Mt 4:23). He is the same Jesus who promised his disciples, "Peace I leave with you; my peace I give to you" (Jn 14:27). If we are available to him, open to him as Savior and Lord, not fighting him but prepared for him to have his way with us, then we are within the healing peace of God which Jesus came to bring to us.

The word *if* is, of course, of paramount importance. It is only *if* we are available to Jesus, open to him as Savior and Lord, that we can expect God's healing peace. You may wish to turn back to chapter two and reaffirm the prayer of response. Once this prayer is your own, you can claim the Son's promise of the Father's peace.

3. There is a common error concerning the peace of God. We tend to think of it as something rather precarious which we have to strive hard to hold and keep or else it will slip away, rather like a piece of slippery soap in the bathtub. Actually, the biblical picture is precisely the opposite. "The peace of God, which surpasses all understanding, will guard your hearts and your minds through Christ Jesus" (Phil 4:7).

We do not keep the peace of God. The peace of God keeps us. So the mental picture I suggest for this meditation is that of yourself surrounded by the ring of God's peace. There is no need to strive. Just rest in the knowledge that it is so.

4. There is another common error: thinking of the peace of God as a weak, passive experience. But the peace of God is no mere absence of turmoil. It is strong and active and vibrant

with life. It must be so, because it is an attribute of God himself. A common title of God in the New Testament is "the God
of Peace." The peace of God is one with the power of God and
the love of God and the joy of God. To be within God's ring
of peace is to be in contact with God's power and love and joy.
It is a place of creativity, a place of healing.

5. So there is no need to do anything. Just "go flop" before
the Lord. Acknowledge his peace. Enjoy his peace. Let his
peace flow around you. Let his peace flow into you—warm,
strong and life-giving.

There is no hurry. You can rest in this place of healing as
long as you choose to do so. You can actually feel the peace
of God entering into every part of your mind, every part of your
body, the very depths of your spirit. You can know that sin and
tension and sickness must retreat before it.

6. When the time is right, bring others into the ring of peace.
It may sound selfish that we should delay bringing the
needs of others to God until our own needs are being met by
God's peace. Yet we cannot bring others into the ring of
peace until we are within it ourselves. Once within the ring,
though, we can offer effective healing prayer without strain or
drain. Both we and the people we pray for should feel the
benefit.

So now, picture your family within the ring of peace. Lift up
each member into that peace. Thank God that it's his will that
your home should be a place of his peace and that peace
should undergird all the relationships of family life. Within the
ring of peace we thank God for this, and let his will flow
through our prayer.

7. Then bring into the ring of peace any other people who
are ill or in trouble. In each case do not concentrate on the

illness or the trouble. Think of each person as someone created and loved by God, a person for whom God's will is wholeness. Let your prayer reinforce God's will as you picture yourself and the one for whom you are praying within the ring of
peace. Again, do not strive or worry or tense up. Let God's own
peace do God's own work.

8. In our Service of Healing, we imagine the ring of peace
growing larger and larger. After picturing our individual selves
within the ring of God's peace, we encircle the whole congregation, all of us in church—our families too—with that same
ring of peace. We thank God for each other. We thank God for
himself in our midst. We thank God that his presence and his
peace are not passive, but actively at work in that moment, full
of purpose and power.

Then we bring within the ring of peace all those for whom
we have been asked to pray, all those whose names are, or
should be, in our intercession book. We read no list of names
and ailments, but simply align our prayers with God's holy and
healing will, offering ourselves as channels of that will for
peace and wholeness.

As a symbol of this prayer, I usually lift and hold the intercession book as we pray. Then we picture the ring of peace
around our neighborhood, then around our country, then en-
circling our world, and finally surrounding the whole universe,
known and unknown.

"Your holy and healing will be done," we pray, and we thank
God that we can offer this prayer with confidence. The will of
the almighty and eternal God must ultimately triumph, his
peace must prevail, his kingdom will come—because he is
God. So these are strong prayers, not weak prayers. We can
offer them not with anxiety, but with calm expectancy.

Practicing the Presence

Our next method of "resting prayer" for healing is a meditation on the practice of the presence of the Living Christ. It begins in much the same way as the ring of peace.

1. Remember that Jesus is with you. As Pope John Paul II has said, "We are an Easter people, and Hallelujah is our song." Jesus is living and available to us. We claim his promise to be with us always (Mt 28:20). When we pray, we assume his real presence.

So picture him—the Lord of healing love. He looks at you and you look at him. Enjoy the privilege of his presence.

2. But remember that the love in his eyes is not sentimental or indulgent. He sees us just as we are, and he has paid the price of crucifixion to be with us. Never forget the cost of Christ's loving presence. We have caused our crucified Savior inconceivable pain, but he has never abandoned us, because he knows he is our only hope.

3. This living sacrificial love of Jesus is radiant and vibrant with God's own healing and re-creating power. Picture his gaze. Feel his hands upon you. Know that his will is for your whole-ness in body, mind and spirit. He never refused the ministry of healing to anyone who came to him. Rest in his changeless will for your healing. Feel him doing you good.

4. Remember that spiritual healing is like physical healing in that sometimes there is not just a hurt to be soothed. Some-thing may need to be cut out or cast out.

So now picture Jesus looking straight into you. He sees clear-ly all that spoils and damages you, any sin, any negativity, any evil or alien element. He "rebukes" it with God's own authority and commands, "Come out of him," "Come out of her."

Let Christ have his way. Try not to resist. He only casts out that which is harmful or worthless. Do not protect it against him. The forces of evil must retreat before him unless we give them sanctuary.

A "mini-exorcism" can take place at the heart of your resting prayer. No elaborate ritual or wild emotion is necessary. All that is needed is the presence of Christ and our cooperation. We should not fear it.

5. Now his hands are on you for healing once again, because maybe the ministry of deliverance was painful for you. Let his love and joy and peace flow about you and into you, stirring God's own life in your body, mind and spirit. Once again, rest in his mighty will for your healing.

6. Now bring into his healing presence any for whom you wish to pray. You do not have to do anything. Picture Jesus. Picture the one for whom you are praying. Bring them together. Just stand by as Jesus looks at your friend, your neighbor, your loved one. Quietly and confidently align your will with that of Jesus, as he speaks to and touches the one for whom you are praying.

Sister Jean Mary of the Community of the Holy Name, who used to be the warden of our diocesan retreat house, says she finds an ideal prayer for healing in John 11:3, the appeal from Martha and Mary to Jesus on behalf of Lazarus: "Lord, he whom you love is ill," or, in another version, "Lord, your dear friend is ill." This prayer looks first at the Lord, then at his love for Lazarus, and only afterward at Lazarus's sickness. This can be our prayer-sequence as we practice the presence of the Living Christ on behalf of others.

7. Finally, the eyes and the hands of Jesus are back on you. It is his will to send you into the world on his behalf. He has something for you to do, and to be, and his hands are upon

you for commissioning, for empowering, for the gift of the Holy Spirit so that you may have whatever resources are needful.

In this sequence of prayer, we have imagined Jesus doing things that we know he did during his earthly ministry. He met people, he understood them and loved them, he exorcised and healed, he commissioned and empowered. We have pictured him doing all these things for us and for those we have brought to him in prayer.

Maybe your mental picture will go further. Perhaps more personal elements will emerge in the ministry of Christ to you and your loved ones. This is to be encouraged. It is sometimes known as the Ignatian method of prayer. It is a sign that the Lord is taking hold of your imagination and using it for his purpose. It is a way in which he equips us for Christian life and work.

So go in peace and serve the Lord. In the name of Christ, Amen.

The Healing Spirit

In our third method of healing prayer, we turn to the Third Person of the Holy Trinity. This prayer is a meditation on the healing work of God the Holy Spirit, but it begins, as in the case of the other two, with some words of Jesus.

1. Recollect the promise of Jesus: "If you then, who are evil, know how to give good gifts to your children, how much more will the heavenly Father give the Holy Spirit to those who ask him!" (Lk 11:13).

2. All who put their faith in Jesus as Lord and Savior may, and should, claim this promise. Otherwise, our Christianity will be tragically incomplete.

The gift of the Holy Spirit has been God's deep purpose for

us since creation. In the words of St. Athanasius, "God has shared our manhood that we might share his Godhead." Jesus promised his disciples, "The Spirit of truth . . . will be in you" (Jn 14:17). He actually commands his followers, "Receive the Holy Spirit" (Jn 20:22).

Just as being a Christian involves taking God the Father on trust from Jesus, so it involves taking on trust God the Holy Spirit. If, in your own life, you have decided that Jesus is to be trusted, then his promise of the Holy Spirit is also to be trusted. Claim the promise. Obey the command. Thank God for the fact of the Holy Spirit in *you*.

3. As, with wonder, you recollect that God is *in you,* remember that the Holy Spirit is the Lord and giver of life. Feel and enjoy the life of God surging in you. Make a mental act of assent and cooperation with the life of God in you—the life of God stirring in every cell of your body, the life of God sharpening and enlightening your mind, the life of God fitting your spirit for eternal life. The God within calls forth your true self, the you that God envisaged since the beginning of time. Say "yes" to your true self.

4. The life of God in you stirs and moves with God's own strength and God's own goodness. Picture the life of God in you, gently but inevitably nudging aside all that is alien to your true self, all that hurts or spoils your body, mind or spirit. Relax and let the God within have his way with you.

Note that again this is a "resting" mode of prayer. God the Holy Spirit does all the work. All we have to do is to let him do it.

5. The life of God within you is one with the ring of God's peace around you and the healing Lord, who has introduced you to both Father and Spirit. Also, the Holy Spirit in you is one

with the Holy Spirit in those who are around you.

Recollect Jesus' prayer to the Father for all believers—"That they may be one, as we are one, I in them and you in me, that they may become completely one" (Jn 17:22-23). Pray for the Church of God, that it may be active and alive by its oneness with the Holy Spirit. Picture your own church being led by the Holy Spirit into life and love and truth and healing power. Offer this mental picture to God in simple trust.

Picture the life of God in every person for whom you feel called to pray. There is no person to whom the life of God is completely alien. Thank God that his life is good, and again in simple trust pray that God may have his own healing and saving way in all his creatures.

Note how positive this method of prayer has been. There has been little agonizing about ailments. It is not that we have denied their existence; it's just that there has been more important business on the prayer agenda. We have looked at God twice as much as we have looked at ourselves or anyone else. We have made an act of faith in God's goodness, God's power, God's involvement in life. As in the case of the other methods of resting prayer, this meditation on the healing work of the Holy Spirit should leave us feeling refreshed.

6. Finally, wait upon the Holy Spirit in silence for some moments. The Father has something for you to do and to be. The Holy Spirit in you is one with the Father and knows his will for you. And he has the necessary gifts and resources for that will to be done through you. Be still, and know the purpose and the power of the kingdom of God within you.

7. Then go in the power of that same Holy Spirit—who is true God and calls you into your true self. Touch the world for healing.

I have experienced union with the

eternal. And so I possess

a cordial which secures me from dying

of thirst in the desert of life.

[ALBERT SCHWEITZER]

—NINE—

HOW DO YOU PRAY WHEN YOU ARE NOT GETTING BETTER?

*T*here is no such thing as a "no-go area" in the practice of healing prayer. So if this book is going to be honest in facing the challenge of how to pray effectively amid life's various experiences and the emotions they generate, we must not flinch from the hard question that follows naturally from the one we asked in the last chapter. How should we pray when we are faced, not just with illness, but with illness that seems chronic or terminal?

I want to suggest a twelve-point prayer-program to meet the challenge of that question.

1. I believe that everything in chapter eight remains applicable regardless of the severity or duration of an illness. In fact, the longer and more painful an illness is, the more important it is to practice the presence of God. The three methods of resting prayer, which I hope by now you have tried for yourself and made your own, will never be inappropriate, and it is good to augment them with other aids to prayer.

Different people are led into God's presence in different ways. It's important to know what works for you. It may be a special Bible passage, like some of the famous verses in John's Gospel in which Jesus describes his nature and his work: "I am the good shepherd" (Jn 10:14); "I am the light of the world" (Jn 8:12); "I am the resurrection and the life" (Jn 11:25). Or it could be an inspirational passage from Paul's writings, such as Romans 8:38-39. Or perhaps there is a well-loved hymn that leads you into the presence of God.

It is well worth taking the time to delve into your hymnbook and make your own choice. I am amazed, for instance, at how much distilled wisdom and devotional aid Bishop Christopher Wordsworth has managed to incorporate into the two verses of this tiny hymn:

> Lord, be thy word my rule,
> In it may I rejoice;
> Thy glory be my aim,
> Thy holy will my choice;
>
> Thy promises my hope,
> Thy providence my guard,
> Thine arms my strong support,
> Thyself my great reward.

"The Word of God," says Bishop Wordsworth, "is a measuring device for life." His hymn helps us to embrace and rejoice in that Word and then goes on to provide a guide for Christian perspective. The brevity and concentration of the language are quite remarkable.

Life's best aim—the glory of God.
Life's best choice—the will of God.
Life's best hope—the promises of God.
Life's best guard—the providence of God.
Life's best support—the strong arm of God.
Life's supreme reward—God himself.

As I pray the words of this hymn, I find that in eight short lines Bishop Wordsworth leads me straight into God's presence.

Another hymn-writer who helps me with the practice of the presence of God is Henry Francis Lyte. His paraphrase of Psalm 103, "Praise, My Soul, the King of Heaven," is a devotional feast, as is, of course, the original psalm.

You may find that in your own case pictures are more valuable than words in leading you into an awareness of God. You might use a photo of a beautiful scene or a reproduction of a lovely painting.

God is a great road-builder. Jesus is the supreme Way, but once we have found him there are innumerable routes to his throne. When you have found your own, treasure the knowledge, employ it well to approach him, and rest in his presence.

2. If you have a serious health problem, admit the fact to God. This doesn't mean accepting that the illness is God's will, but that it is a fact of life at the moment.

It does no honor to God to pretend that illness does not exist. I recently attended a Christian healing conference at which one of the participants was not at all well. Some of the other participants seemed determined to pretend that there was nothing wrong with him. They urged him to think positively and praise God. This didn't make him feel better. It just made him feel guilty about his illness!

We sometimes wish for a magic wand that could be waved over the sick with a total and automatic guarantee of an instant cure. But the ministry of Christian healing provides no such magic wand. If Jesus had had one, he would have waved it over the scribes and Pharisees and healed their hardness of heart. He would have waved it in Nazareth, where his powers were restricted because people did not believe in him because he was a local boy (Mt 13:53-58).

I have to admit to being suspicious of speakers or writers who give the impression of a 100 percent success rate in their ministry of healing. My guess is that further investigation would reveal a great deal of selectivity and not a little wishful thinking in their reporting. It is surely better to be absolutely honest when we talk to God or to each other.

3. Having identified a health problem, take it to Jesus—or rather, take yourself to Jesus. The Ignatian method of prayer, mentioned in the last chapter, may be helpful here. Read any of the Gospel stories about Jesus. Picture the scene—its sights, noises, smells and textures. Allow your imagination to bring the story to life. Then, in your mind, become part of it. Approach Jesus, just as you are.

4. It's important to want Jesus *for himself,* not just for the by-products that come when we meet him. But there always are by-products in the lives of those who meet him and love him and trust him. Some of them can be spectacular, and so . . .

5. Be prepared for surprises! Jesus continually sprang surprises on the people of his day. Peter, Andrew, James and John

must have been surprised to find themselves leaving the family fishing business and following Jesus (Mt 4:18-22). Matthew must have been surprised to find himself leaving his lucrative tax-collecting office and becoming the disciple of a carpenter (Mt 9:9-13).

Everybody was surprised when Jesus stilled a storm at sea with just a word (Lk 8:22-25). They were surprised, too, when he stilled the storm in the mind of the violent madman in the graveyard at Gerasa (Lk 8:26-39). The professional mourners who were called in to weep and wail at the funeral of Jairus' daughter were totally devastated when the little girl they were sure was dead got up and walked around after ministry by Jesus (Mk 5:35-43).

There was no end to the surprises—and not the least of them was the discovery by the disciples that the healing ministry was placed in their hands also (Lk 9:1-6; 10:1-23).

The surprises have not ceased today. They can take many forms in cases of serious illness.

Sometimes, against all the odds, there is a physical change. I think of Norah. I was invited to her home to pray and lay hands on her after hospital administrators had decided that her cancer was inoperable and that it would be better for her to die at home. She made an instant, total recovery—though the family had been told she had only a few days to live. Quite a surprise for them all! And for me, too, because I did not learn of her healing till seven years later, when I met her husband again.

Sometimes there is only a partial physical healing, or no physical healing at all. But there is still a surprise—a mental or spiritual change that is just as remarkable as a physical healing. I think of Jenny, who was told that she, like Norah, had terminal cancer. She came month by month to the healing service at our parish church. Over the months, she and her husband traveled hundreds of miles so that they could worship with us. She certainly was open to physical healing, and I longed that she should have it, but gradually her physical condition deteriorated. Yet as her body weakened, her spirit gained strength; as her body faded, her spirit shone.

Though Jenny's experience was not the same as Norah's, it would be wrong to say that in Jenny's case there was no healing.

Sometimes the surprise takes the form of a blessing for the people around the one who is sick. They grow in understanding, faith and commitment, when logically the very opposite should be happening. Gerald had to watch his little daughter die. Afterward, when he might have been excused for cursing God, he found himself giving his life to Christ and offering himself for the ministry.

Or the surprise could be that somehow, mysteriously, God uses a thoroughly wretched and undesirable situation for his own loving purposes. He brings good out of evil. The supreme example has to be the crucifixion of Jesus. It was a vile event. Yet God used it to redeem the world.

So be prepared for surprises. Avoid rigidity of thought—both the rigidity of faithlessness that says, "Things are hopeless, all is lost, my situation is beyond help," and the rigidity that masquerades as faith, but is actually a rather presumptuous attempt to dictate to God: "Healing will take place on my terms and according to my timetable." Either kind of rigidity is a block to healing. Much better is an attitude of flexible availability and openness to God, believing that prayer is never wasted and that God is on our side.

6. Trust may not always come easily. It may be threatened by myriad doubts and difficulties. In that case, it is better to face them than to suppress them.

If you find yourself asking, "Why should this happen to me?" admit the thought, though it may be therapeutic to put the question in a different form—"If suffering is a fact in this world, why should I be exempt?" If you still find yourself becoming angry with God, admit the feeling, and rage against him if you must. Remember chapter three: God accepts and bears our anger.

7. Know that God understands suffering from the inside. It is part of the message of the cross that if we find ourselves treading the road of pain, God the Son will be our companion on the way, our sustainer and our fellow-sufferer.

8. Look for some valid reason to be thankful. Thankfulness does us good, and we need that good especially when times are hard. Thankfulness kindles a tiny light in the gloom, and as Confucius said, "It is better to light a candle than to curse the darkness."

9. If there is something in your life that you need to confess and make amends for, do it. The confession of sin is important, both for its own sake and also because an unconfessed sin can be a contributory factor in sickness.

10. Find some other person, or persons, to pray for. It is good to remove our minds from our own troubles, and prayers from the heart of suffering do seem to have a particular strength.

11. Listen for practical guidance from God. Is there something you should be doing for yourself? For instance, are you receiving the right sort of medical care? Are you receiving the church's healing ministry to the full? Is there something you

should be doing for someone else? A gift to offer? An apology to make? An insight to share? A relationship to repair?

12. Then go right back to stage one. Rest in the love of God for you. Do not bring your prayer to an end; make it cyclical. Let it merge into the whole of your life. Keep looking forward. As a Christian, you can know that in life or death the best is yet to be.

Much of this twelve-stage prayer-sequence is illustrated by the true story of a man to whom I had the privilege of ministering for many years. Let's call him Roger.

When I first met Roger, he was a sick man. There were so many things wrong with him that I wouldn't know how to begin to describe his condition. Before long he was spending half his life in hospital, undergoing operation after operation. The medical treatment was almost as great a trial to him as his underlying condition. His Christian faith was severely tested by it all.

Then one day there was an emergency call from the hospital to the vicarage. My wife was told that Roger was dying. He was in a private ward, wired to various sorts of medical gadgets that were monitoring his condition. They showed that he could not have more than an hour or so to live. Many of his vital functions were stopping or had stopped.

Unfortunately, I was out and could not be reached, but my wife phoned one of our curates, and he rushed to the hospital, anointed Roger and gave him Holy Communion. Then the first miracle took place.

As Roger was anointed for healing in the name of Jesus, unaccountably the medical gadgetry around him showed that his vital functions had returned to working order. The nurses were amazed as they watched the screen beside his bed record the healing process.

Roger went on to live for a further six years, which made a second miracle possible. Though much of the time he was confined to a wheelchair, and he had many problems and much pain, there was a transformation in his spirit. His personal Christianity grew and deepened. His faith underwent a renewal. I continued to visit him—but now as much for my own sake as for his.

He mapped out a practical program of work. He was an architectural writer, and he set himself new goals and fulfilled them.

Then one day, he sent for me and told me he believed he had only a week to live. He asked me to prepare him a seven-day prayer schedule, so that the week would not be wasted. He planned his funeral in detail, and, though the service he designed made no attempt to disguise the pain and the problems he had faced, it was full of faith, joy and gratitude to God for life, thanks to his widowed father for all his loving care, and an almost excited readiness to embark on the great adventure that lay ahead.

Seven days later, having completed his prayer schedule, he died a "healed death."

The church was packed for his funeral. People came from many miles away to show their affection and respect, and we were all able to benefit from Roger's wisdom and courage in death, just as we had often benefited from his wisdom and courage in life.

His father had found it difficult not to feel bitter about Roger's suffering, but as I write I am conscious of a new strength and depth and loveliness in his Christian faith too.

Somehow nothing was wasted in the years of chronic illness

Roger underwent. And now I believe with all my heart that he is with his Savior, leaping and running and exploring eternity. Unhampered by the disabilities that dogged his earthly life, Roger is rejoicing in the architecture of heaven, where God will wipe away all tears and "death will be no more; mourning and crying and pain will be no more, for the first things have passed away" (Rev 20:4).

None has made himself master of

terrors save Christ, who has conquered

Death and all temporal

evils—even eternal death.

[*MARTIN LUTHER*]

— TEN —

HOW DO YOU
PRAY IN
BEREAVEMENT?

*E*verybody undergoes the experience of bereavement sooner or later. The first experience may be when our grandparents die, and then our parents. Fifty percent of married people experience the loss of their partners. This can be devastating if the marriage was healthy and intimate. Then, too, most of us lose a close friend at one time or another. One of my own close friends died at a very early age after an auto accident.

It may be that at this moment you are yourself suffering bereavement, or someone close to you is doing so. How can prayer bring healing into the pain of this experience?

I believe there are three principal elements in healing prayer at a time of bereavement.

First, it's essential to mourn adequately—not to bottle up the complex feelings that come to us at these times, but to allow them to well up and spill out.

I remember attending the funeral of a well-loved church sexton when I was a teenager. The vicar's opening words, spoken in a bluff and hearty voice, were, "We are not here today to grieve but to rejoice!" Of course he meant that Christians have the privilege of claiming the promise of the gospel and know that life in Christ is stronger in death. But we all felt an almost physical sense of shock at his words—both on our own behalf and on behalf of the sexton's wife.

When I became a vicar myself, I did something almost as silly. I went into a house where the family was in mourning and the curtains were all closed as a sign of their grief. With extraordinary insensitivity, I went from room to room pulling the curtains open as I spoke of the Christian doctrine of eternal life. It was not until I had almost finished that I noticed the pain on the faces around me. I cringe now to think of it.

It is a basic principle of pastoral care that to help people in trouble, you have to put yourself in the place where they are and allow them to be themselves and to express what is in them. The prophet Ezekiel showed the heart of a true pastor when he visited the exiles at Tel-abib. Overcome by what he saw, he said very little; in his own words, he just "sat there among them for seven days" (Ezek 3:15).

What is true of good pastoral care is also true of effective healing prayer.

When we are bereaved we can go to God, just as we are. The coming of Jesus into this world reminds us that we have a God who "sits among us." The first step in healing prayer is to avoid any pretense in his presence.

There is great wisdom in Joseph Scriven's hymn "What a Friend We Have in Jesus." In bereavement, as in so many of life's troubles, it is a Christian's healing privilege "to carry *everything* to God in prayer."

The "everything" that we bring to God in prayer at a time of bereavement will differ from person to person. It will depend on individual circumstances and also on the time that has elapsed since the actual death.

In the early days of bereavement, the main feeling may paradoxically be a lack of feeling. It is as though nature mercifully anesthetizes us for a while. There may well be a numbness of mind and spirit. It may be difficult to believe that the bereavement has happened. Even though to lose someone who is dear and close brings loneliness and grief, it's common in the early stages to feel that the situation is somehow unreal. There is almost a sense of shock when we come home and the loved one is not there to welcome us. These feelings need to be brought to God.

A little later it's common for the numbness to be superseded by confusion and disorientation. Powers of concentration may be lost. The memory may play tricks, so that we cannot spell simple words or recall well-known names. This is often accompanied by feelings of exhaustion. Little things can tire us out. Reserves of energy can be quickly drained. Sometimes there can be feelings of fearfulness in the face of activities or events that had never bothered us in the past.

All of this should also be brought to God. Gradually, disorientation will be superseded by reorientation. This is a sign that we are beginning to recover, but often it does not feel so, because with reorientation can come feelings of guilt and resentment. It is not unusual to feel anger toward any we may feel have failed us, or even toward the deceased person for having presumed to die and leave us alone! We must also be prepared for feelings of anger against God of the sort that were described in chapter three.

We may know that many of our feelings are not reasonable, but this will not prevent them from being strong. Maybe we will feel that others are avoiding us or are unwilling to speak about our bereavement—and this indeed could be true. Again, all of these experiences and feelings must be brought before God.

There may be a problem with persistent grief months and even years after the bereavement. There may well be depression, even a temporary loss of the will to live. None of this is abnormal, but it's important that we not bear it alone. We should not hesitate to share our feelings with those who are close to us or to ask for counseling and care in church.

Above all, we must be our real selves in the presence of God. Unreal prayer will yield no real results. Honesty must be the first item on the healing-prayer agenda.

But honesty is not the *only* item. Prayer is a two-way conversation. After we have vented all our pain and anger and confusion in God's presence, we will find that as we stand drained and empty before him, it is his will not only to share our grief but also to begin to fill our emptiness. This is the second phase of healing prayer in time of bereavement.

Jesus had so much to teach about life and death, time and eternity. All through his ministry he taught that God the Father did not design human life to terminate at the point of physical death. Life is a journey. Death is a frontier post. Beyond it is a mysterious new dimension.

One day we will all stand at the threshold of that mystery.

It is right to be in awe at the thought of it, but Jesus promises us that if we stand there with our hand in his hand and our trust in his saving power, we may stand completely without fear.

The Gospels of Matthew, Mark, Luke and John all record many words of Jesus about life after death. For instance, Matthew preserves Christ's command to us to store up "treasures in heaven" (Mt 6:20). Mark records the promise that those who make sacrifices for the sake of Christ will receive "in the age to come eternal life" (Mk 10:30). Luke tells us that the children of the resurrection "cannot die any more, because they are like angels and are children of God" (Lk 20:36). John preserves for us the precious assurance that "God so loved the world that he gave his only Son, so that everyone who believes in him may not perish but may have everlasting life" (Jn 3:16).

With his dying breath Jesus reiterated this teaching as he promised the penitent thief, "Today you will be with me in Paradise" (Lk 23:43).

After his death, everything Jesus had taught was gloriously vindicated and exemplified by his own resurrection from the dead. Christians believe if we put our hand into his hand, he will lead us the way he has himself already traveled—through this life into death, and beyond death into the mystery of eternity—and he invites us to accept that wherever we travel with him we may have quiet confidence that in his presence there is no cause for fearfulness; instead, there is every reason for assurance and anticipation.

If these things have been explained to us long before we undergo bereavement, we have a reservoir of hope, and sooner or later we will find healing truth gently flowing into us from that reservoir. Words long since committed to memory will resurface with new meaning and relevance.

"Even though I walk through the valley of the shadow of death, I fear no evil, for you are with me" (Ps 23:4). Yes, of course death casts a shadow, and the valley of the shadow is a gloomy place to be. But a shadow cannot actually harm us. The shadow of a bee cannot sting. The shadow of a dog cannot bite. We have a resource in bereavement that prevents the gloom from degenerating into the fearfulness of total darkness.

"I fear no evil, *for you are with me.*" If we know anything of Jesus as Savior and Lord, we will find ourselves reaching out to him and finding that he has not abandoned us. The one who went to the cross and rose from the grave is with us in bereavement, and where Jesus is, there is his power to love and to heal.

If our loved one was a committed Christian, we shall find ourselves claiming the great biblical promise of John 3:16 on his or her behalf. "God so loved the world that he gave his only Son, so that John or Mary—my friend, my loved one, who was a believer—may not perish but may have everlasting life." We will realize that while it may be natural to grieve for ourselves, we need not grieve for those we've lost. As far as they are concerned, life must be better than ever.

What if John or Mary was not, as far as we know, a committed Christian? We must not fabricate false expectations. There will be no comfort for us in that. But there are many key Christian truths we can still affirm.

We can rest in the knowledge of the nature of God, who made us and loves us. All of us are of value and concern to God. When those who are dear to us pass from our sight, they do not pass from his sight.

God made John and Mary. He loves them—more than we can. He understands them—better than we have ever done.

God has always wanted them for himself, and still does.

Of course, the Bible speaks of hell as well as heaven. I wish this were not so, but it is. Nevertheless, God is strong and wise and good, and as he works out the eternal destiny of John and Mary, he does so in a way that is entirely consistent with his strength and wisdom and goodness. They could not be in better hands than the hands of the God and Father of our Lord Jesus Christ. It is our privilege to place them in those hands in our prayers and then to leave them there trustfully, knowing that they are more precious to God than they have ever been to us.

After we have poured out all our feelings in God's presence and allowed him to begin to fill our emptiness, there is still a third phase if we are to experience Christian healing in bereavement. The time will come when we will begin to realize that we still have a future on earth as well as a future in heaven, and it is right that we commit that future to the God who still has something for us to do and be in his service.

We cannot force or hasten the moment when we are ready to accept the future and let life go on, but when it comes we should not resist it. As we practice the presence of God day by day, we will find that problems can be tackled with his help one by one, and life can be lived a day at a time.

We should be gentle with ourselves during our rehabilitation. Realizing that we are genuinely hurt people, we need not be ashamed to spoil ourselves just a little. We will find in time that our feelings of self-pity will diminish, and we need not be afraid to congratulate ourselves when we find we're starting to think about ways of helping others, rather than dwelling on our own need to be helped.

If we are wise we will not rush into big decisions, but we'll find ourselves taking increasing interest in the little ones. We will look after our health and appearance and diet because we know that God would want this, and so would our loved one. We won't allow ourselves to feel guilty if we are surprised by moments of pleasure and happiness—perhaps connected with an old interest or a new one. When the time comes for us to face a big decision, we will work out the pros and cons, take sensible advice, say our prayers and step forward into life knowing that God has no intention of allowing us to waste it.

To summarize, then: The first phase of healing prayer in a time of bereavement is to allow ourselves to mourn with total honesty, knowing that our emotions are better out than in, and that whatever our feelings may be, God invites us to bring them to him and to vent them into his bosom. In the second phase, when we have emptied ourselves of our griefs and emotions, we should allow the gospel of the crucified and risen Christ to enter into us so that he can begin to do his own loving work in his own healing way. Third, we can allow God's healing truth and love to start to rehabilitate us.

We may find these things happening consecutively. We may find them happening simultaneously. We may move from one phase to another erratically. We may make up our own prayers, or we may find prayers that others have composed but that speak to and for us in a special way. Let me share such a prayer with you as we come to the end of this chapter.

Not long ago I was asked by our local radio station to devise and present a program on the subject of bereavement. The producer of the program had himself recently been bereaved; his wife had died of cancer. I asked him whether he could bear to be interviewed during the course of the program about his own experience and feelings. Very courageously, he agreed.

One of the questions I put to him was about prayer. Had he

found any help through prayer? And if so, what sort of prayer had helped him most?

When I asked him this, he produced from his pocket a battered piece of paper. "This prayer," he said, "has brought me more help than anything else." He put it in my hand and asked me to read it to the listeners.

Our local radio station does not cover a very large area, yet the response to that prayer was remarkable. Immediately a hundred listeners wrote in asking for a copy It had struck a chord in their experience, and they wanted the help and hope it offered.

Wondering why the producer's prayer touched so many people, I realized that it embodied all the principles we have dealt with in this chapter. Our three themes are set side by side in it, simply and beautifully.

Since I found this prayer, I have passed it on to hundreds of mourners. Here it is—either for your own use, or for you to share with another

Lord, the trouble about life just now is that I seem to have all the things which don't matter and to have lost all the things which do matter. I have life; I have money to live on; I have plenty to occupy me; but I am alone, and sometimes I feel that nothing can make up for that.

Lord, compel me to see the meaning of my faith. Make me believe that I have a hope as well as a memory, that the unseen cloud of witnesses is around me and that you meant it when you said you would always be with me.

Make me to realize that as long as you leave me here, there is something I am meant to do, and, in doing it, help me to find the comfort and the courage I need to go on. Through Jesus, my Lord and Master, Amen.

Lord, teach us to pray.

[A DISCIPLE]

—ELEVEN—

THE LORD'S OWN METHOD OF PRAYER

*I*n considering methods of healing prayer, perhaps we have so far missed the most important and the most obvious of them all. There is one and only one method of prayer that has come to us direct from Jesus himself. We tend to neglect it because we know it so well, and though familiarity has not exactly bred contempt, we sometimes find ourselves forgetting its depth and power.

This prayer method has been preserved for us in Matthew 6:9-13 and Luke 11:1-4. According to Luke, the disciples were motivated to ask Jesus for help with prayer when they saw him at prayer himself. He replied to their request with a command: "When [not *if*] you pray, say . . ." And then he taught them the sequence of phrases that we know as the Lord's Prayer. It is remarkable not only for its devotional wisdom but also, I believe, for its healing potential.

The Lord's Prayer repays detailed, word-by-word study. Let's delve into some of its riches now.

Father. The Lord's Prayer takes us straight into the heart of the experience of Christian healing. All relationships have a profound effect upon our health of body, mind and spirit. Good relationships have a good effect; bad relationships have a bad effect. St. Augustine benefited from a good mother, but Adolf Hitler suffered from a cruel father. Their lives bore the marks of these fundamental relationships.

It is the claim of the Christian faith that through Jesus Christ we can enjoy a good relationship of awe-inspiring magnitude—a wonderful relationship with the Almighty himself. Through Jesus we are privileged to address the Cosmic Creator as "Father." Those whom Jesus calls "brothers and sisters" become the adopted sons and daughters of his Father.

Matthew preserves an important additional word in his opening to the Lord's Prayer. The word is "our." Healing prayer should be a corporate experience. God is not just Father; he is *our* Father. Christians are called into a family. A cold, remote church made up of independent individuals who keep to themselves would be a travesty. The healing relationship of which we remind ourselves at the outset of the Lord's Prayer not only is with God but should also be with our brothers and sisters in the family of God.

The prayer continues—*in heaven.* This reminds us that God's nature is the highest and the best. It is a warning that we must not make God too small.

We shrink God all too easily. It is a psychological process

known as projection. Just as a film projector casts an image of whatever is in it onto an outside screen, so, too, our minds tend to project our own feelings and emotions onto those around us. For example, a mean man will tend to read mean motives into the actions of those around him. In the same way, we sometimes project our human feelings and failings into our concept of God.

The Lord's Prayer is a healthy corrective. "Heaven" is the word that describes God's own deep and distinctive nature. His nature is infinitely and breathtakingly beyond us—and yet it is a paradox of the Christian healing ministry that here and now, by the grace of God, we are meant to begin to enter heaven, and heaven is meant to begin to enter us.

Hallowed be your name. In the Bible, a name is not just a "tag" by which one is known. In Hebrew thought, one's name is somehow part of one's nature. Hallowing God's name means holding everything connected with God in deep honor. True prayer, says Jesus, involves reverencing God and filling our minds and hearts with the qualities that reflect his nature.

Paul gives good healing advice in Philippians 4:8: "Beloved, whatever is true, whatever is honorable, whatever is just, whatever is pure, whatever is pleasing, whatever is commendable, if there is any excellence and if there is anything worthy of praise, think about these things." All too often we feed our minds on garbage, and then we wonder why we are neither happy nor healthy!

Your kingdom come. The kingdoms of greed, lust and hate are all sick realms. God's perfect kingdom will be a state of perfect wholeness. Healing worship both proclaims and claims the benefits of the kingdom. Every experience of Christian healing is a breaking through of God's kingdom into ours.

Your will be done. We now come to what is arguably the most misunderstood phrase in the Bible. "Thy will be done" is not a sigh of resignation ("I accept my cancer"). It is a battle cry: "Let your holy and healing will prevail over all else, rebuking all that is alien to the perfection of your creative purpose, cleansing, purging, re-creating, making whole."

We know that the will of God is for our wholeness in body, mind and spirit because Jesus *never* refused the ministry of healing to anyone. But to reinforce our confidence, the Lord's Prayer adds "on earth *as it is in heaven,"* where, as we know, God will wipe away all tears, there will be no more death, and "mourning and crying and pain will be no more" (Rev 21:4). So we pray, "Triumph, Lord, over sin and sickness and everything that has no place in your perfect plan." We affirm God's will and rest in it.

Give us this day our daily bread. We pray for the right food for our bodies—and ask ourselves, "Can I share my eating and drinking pattern with Jesus?" We pray for the right food for our minds—and ask ourselves, "Can I share my thought patterns with Jesus?" We pray for the right food for our souls—and ask, "Is Jesus the heart of my worship and spiritual life?"

And forgive us our debts. Guilt can be an element in sickness. It is important to ask and to trust that we have received forgiveness in the name of Jesus.

I well remember "Jasmine," a lady who for years had endured a cumbersome surgical collar and was often in pain. As we talked, she was moved to tell me of a sin she had committed many years before. "Every night," she said, "before I go to sleep, I plead with God for forgiveness for that sin."

It was a joy to be able to tell her the good news about God's gift of forgiveness through Jesus Christ and to offer this prayer-prescription to her: "Tonight, before you go to sleep, ask once more for forgiveness, but do so quite specifically in the name of Jesus, who died on the cross to be your Savior and to bring you forgiveness fully, freely and forever. Then tomorrow, don't ask for forgiveness for that sin again. If you feel you must mention it, just say, 'Thank you, God, for forgiving me my sin.' And the next night and the night after, and as long as you think it necessary, just say, 'Thank you, God, that you *have* forgiven me through Jesus Christ.' "

Within two weeks, Jasmine had discarded her surgical collar and was free from pain. It had taken its leave along with her guilt and stress.

As we also have forgiven our debtors. Forgiving and being forgiven go together, like the "heads" and "tails" sides of a coin. Jesus says we cannot have one without the other—nor should we want to. In chapters three and four, we already looked at some of the evils that attend the failure to forgive. By contrast, when we learn to pray the Lord's Prayer and to mean it, we may find that learning to forgive brings startling benefits.

These benefits can sometimes be measured in precise medical terms. For instance, in Paul Tournier's book *A Doctor's Casebook in the Light of the Bible,* he tells the story of a woman whose blood count changed suddenly after she had been treated for several months for anemia. Her doctor asked, "Has anything out-of-the-ordinary happened in your life since your last visit?"

She replied, "Yes, I have suddenly been able to forgive someone against whom I bore a nasty grudge."

"Such occurrences," says Dr. Tournier, "are not rare."

And do not bring us to the time of trial. Making allowance for Hebrew idiom, this means, "Don't let us be led into temptation; don't let us be tested beyond our breaking point." It is a healthy sign of honesty to admit our weaknesses and limitations to God, and to ask him to grant us his protection whenever he knows that we need it.

But rescue us from the evil one. Like the prayer of the practice of the presence of the Living Christ in chapter eight, the Lord's Prayer has an element of deliverance within it. We are damaged people. We have been invaded by all sorts of elements and forces that are alien to God's plan and purpose for us. Because Jesus wants the best for us, it is his will that anything that spoils and diminishes us should be cast out.

There are three traditional sources for these invading elements—the world, the flesh (our own sinful nature) and the devil. "Agnes" had an ingrained spirit of resentment because of her experience of the world in general, and of a cruel stepmother in particular. "Brad" had a spirit of lust, which started as a voluntary sin, but developed into an involuntary addiction. "Franchette" experimented with a ouija board for fun, but the spirit of oppression that dogged her afterwards was no laughing matter.

These alien elements, which appeared to derive respectively from the world, the flesh and the devil, were deeply disturbing to the three people involved, but they were expelled totally by the ministry of healing prayer. Evil must retreat before God's word of exorcism, unless we protect it and cuddle it to ourselves. It is good (though painful) to expose our sins to God and to say, "Lord, take them. Deliver us from evil." The scarred and wounded hands of our Savior will receive them and bear them away.

Finally, if we adopt the fuller form of the Lord's Prayer, it leads us into an affirmation of the eternal perspective and a burst of powerful positive thinking as we praise God: *For the kingdom and the power and the glory are yours forever. Amen.*

We can be hoodwinked into thinking that the devil holds all the aces. He does not. He is noisier than God. He is less scrupulous than God. He is a natural liar and a con artist. But, in the last resort, he cannot win.

Evil, though it kills, has death at its heart and will ultimately self-destruct, whereas love, though it dies, has life at its heart and will rise again and triumph. This must be so, if God is God. The Lord's Prayer says yes to the essential nature of things, as does the ministry of Christian healing. We add our own personal assent to the Lord's Prayer when we say "Amen"—"Yes, Lord. So be it."

So here is a prayer to say for ourselves and for others, a prayer to say slowly and thoughtfully, abiding in its wisdom, phrase by phrase, sustained by the closeness it brings to the one who gave it to us.

Hold to Christ,

and for the rest be

totally uncommitted.

[HERBERT BUTTERFIELD]

TWELVE

JESUS MAKES
A DIFFERENCE

*I*f I had to select a single phrase to summarize the message of this book, I think I would choose the simple words of the title of this chapter—"Jesus makes a difference." If you prefer to have it in a more scriptural form, there are the words of Paul in 2 Corinthians 5:17, "If anyone is in Christ, there is a new creation." There could hardly be a greater difference than that!

Ordinary folk, whether they have an interest in religion or not, know deep in their bones that something is wrong with this world and that something needs to change. They turn on the TV and the evidence is on the screen before them—the warfare, the violence, the suffering caused by tyrants and terrorists, needless famines, the AIDS problem, the drug problem, the problems of crime and vandalism, the threat of pollution, the threat of nuclear war. The list is endless. These are all problems caused by humankind, and, if the planet is to survive, somehow things need to be different.

Indeed, ordinary folk do not need to turn on the TV to know that things need to be different. The sorts of problems we have been dealing with in this book (guilt, shame, anger, depression, anxiety, fearfulness, stress, jealousy, sickness and the many other forms of suffering) are so common that our own lives tell us that things need to be different.

The good news of Christianity is that this difference is not only needed but possible and available through Jesus. Jesus makes a difference, if we give him half a chance.

This comes as something of a surprise to many people in Britain, my homeland. There is a curious British heresy that religion is little more than a hobby, something to do with your spare time. So often we put churchgoing on the same level as playing golf, walking the dog or tinkering with the car. We think it's a nice enough pastime for those who happen to like that sort of thing. Indeed, most of us can feel a vague attachment to the church on special occasions like weddings or christenings or Christmas carol services, but few people would think of the Christian church as the possible source of an earth-shattering change in their lives.

Yet that is exactly how the Christian faith and the Christian church are presented in the New Testament. The teachings of Jesus were revolutionary and controversial in his lifetime. He himself was the supreme man of action. People who encountered him were never the same again. Some were so infuriated by him that they wanted to kill him, and did! But those who allowed him access to their lives found that they became new people. Lepers were cleansed. Demoniacs were delivered. Greedy materialists were brought to repentance. All sorts of people were changed in body, mind and spirit. Physical and mental health, attitudes and relationships were all affected. Lifestyles were often changed beyond all recognition.

This difference that Jesus made—and still makes, if we give him the chance—is the heart and essence of the Christian healing ministry. In the memorable words of Bishop Morris Maddocks, adviser to the archbishops of Canterbury and York in the ministry of Christian healing, "Christian healing is Jesus Christ meeting you at the point of your need." Healing prayer is meeting Jesus and bringing others to meet him—nothing more, nothing less—and letting him make his own characteristic life-saving difference.

If this is so, then certain basic prayer principles follow logically.

Christian healing prayer is never a meditation on sickness, but neither is it a pretense that sickness does not exist. It is not a striving to extract healing from a reluctant God, but neither is it some magical formula that can bend God to our will. It is not "spare-part praying" that concentrates on a damaged organ or a troubled area of life. It is a concern for whole people, and it ranges over the whole of life in the light of the healing power of the gospel of Jesus Christ.

Every part of the gospel message has a practical implication for living and can be the basis for healing prayer. Healing prayer has two possible starting points, both of which have been illustrated in this book. It can begin with a truth about God, as in the three methods of prayer in chapter eight. Or, as we saw in chapter three, it can begin with an honest assessment of a basic situation and then move on to discover the element in the gospel that ministers to that situation. No part of Christian doctrine is irrelevant to life. Every part carries healing in it in one way or another.

The Apostles' Creed provides a good illustration. We can so easily recite it unthinkingly. Yet every ingredient in it can be the basis for prayer and meditation. Each of its statements of belief can be a means by which Jesus makes a healing difference to us and through us.

I believe in God the Father Almighty, maker of heaven and earth. The ministry of healing follows logically if God is Creator. This is a damaged world, and we are damaged people. If God is self-consistent, logic requires that when his creativity encounters something that is damaged, it must reveal itself as *re*-creativity, or healing. It is no surprise that not long after the Bible reveals God as Creator in Genesis 1, it goes on to reveal him as Healer in Exodus 15:26.

If we make real contact with the Father in our corporate worship and our private prayers, this must be a healing experience for us and must have healing implications for those for whom we pray. So it's good to pray, "Great Creator God, grant that we may come by prayer into your re-creative presence and that we may bring others too in the name of Jesus."

I believe in Jesus Christ his only Son, our Lord, who lived, died, rose again and is available to us here and now. Jesus provides both our authority and our resource for healing. Again, simple logic points it out. We have only to ask ourselves four basic questions:

1. Do I believe Jesus healed the sick, that he went about "proclaiming the good news of the kingdom and curing every disease and every sickness among the people" (Mt 4:23)? If the answer to this is yes, then . . .

2. Do I believe that he rose from the dead? If the answer is again yes, then . . .

3. Do I believe that he is "the same yesterday and today and forever" (Heb 13:8)? If once again the answer is yes, then finally . . .

4. Do I believe he meant it when he promised his followers, "I am with you always, to the end of the age" (Mt 28:20)?

If we answer yes to all four questions, we have committed ourselves to the basis of the Christian healing ministry. Our authority is his command, "Proclaim the kingdom of God and heal" (as in Lk 9:2 and 10:9). Our resource is his own promised healing presence. We should not be surprised if being one with him in prayer leads to healing. In fact, we should be surprised if it doesn't!

The Apostles' Creed reminds us of many facets of the life of Jesus—his months in the womb, his birth into the world, his conflict with worldly powers, his death for our salvation, his mysterious journey into the world of the dead, his triumphant rising again to new life, his eternal kingship and his promised second coming.

Every part of human life is filled with needs. All these needs are met in some aspect of the life of Jesus. For example, the promise of his Second Coming is full of healing. *He shall come to judge the living and the dead.* Never before has the end of this world, as we know it, been such an undisputed scientific possibility. There are three obvious ways in which it could happen. There could be a nuclear explosion, because we have the power of "overkill" and could obliterate our planet many times over. There could be a "disease explosion"—perhaps AIDS or some other equally horrific plague. Or there could be an ecological disaster of mammoth proportions—maybe a catastrophic breaking up of the ozone layer.

The thought of these possibilities could terrify us out of our wits! It could shatter life's purpose and peace—but it will not do anything of the sort, if we listen to the Christian message.

The healing message of the Second Coming is that human sin and stupidity will *not* have the last word in the history of planet earth. Jesus will have it. In fact, Jesus, the Word of God, will *be* it.

Christians have the promise that when this world order comes to an end, we will fall not into the abyss of chaos, but into the arms of Jesus. We have the privilege of watching and praying and resting on the conviction that Christ will come again. Jürgen Moltmann puts it in a nutshell: "Christ is our hope, because Christ is our future." So we join in the words of the ancient prayer preserved in 1 Corinthians 16:22: *Marana tha*—"Our Lord, come!"

I believe in the Holy Spirit. We have already considered the healing implications of the doctrine of God the Holy Spirit in the meditation-prayer at the end of chapter eight. The Old Testament Hebrew word for Spirit is *ruach;* the New Testament Greek word is *pneuma.* The two words have the same basic meaning—"breath" or "wind."

Breath and wind are symbols of life in the Bible. Adam comes to life when God breathes into his nostrils (Gen 2:7). The dead bodies in Ezekiel's vision are brought to life by the wind (Ezek 37:9). In the Acts of the Apostles, the early Christians were filled with new spiritual life when the "rush of a violent wind" of the Holy Spirit came upon them (Acts 2:2).

If we say we believe in the Holy Spirit, we are saying we believe that God's life can move in us in a totally new way, displacing the sick and negative elements in us and empowering us to become the people God created us to be. Every Christian can pray, "Breathe on me, Breath of God, fill me with life anew." "Come Holy Ghost—upon me and upon those for whom I pray." "May the healing power of the Holy Spirit be in us."

I believe in the holy catholic church. When we say we believe in the universal church, we are not just recognizing the fact that the church exists. We are saying that for all its faults, we place our trust in the church as God's instrument. We accept, with Paul, that the church is the "body of Christ" (1 Cor 12:27). We believe the church is called to do the healing work of Christ, speak the healing word of Christ and give the healing touch of Christ.

You and I are called to be part of that healing ministry. In the words of St. Teresa, "Christ has no body now on earth but yours, no hands but yours, no feet but yours. Yours are the eyes through which his compassion must look on the world. Yours are the feet with which he must go about doing good. Yours are the hands with which he must bless men now."

So we may pray, "Lord Jesus Christ, whose body all Christians are called to be, let our prayers come from your heart and accomplish your healing will. Help us to be your body not just in name but in deed and in truth."

I believe in the communion of saints. We are healed or harmed by the company we keep, so what a privilege it is to be called into the "communion of saints." Though this is one of the most neglected Christian doctrines, it is one of the most glorious—and it is certainly full of potential for healing.

All those who put their trust in Jesus are called not only to be one with Jesus but also to be one with each other. We are called to be one with the other members of a local church. The

New Testament knows no such thing as a solitary Christian; in fact, the word *Christian* is never found in the singular in the Bible. We are part of our local family of God; we are also part of the worldwide family of God. When my wife and I travel from England to other parts of the world to conduct Christian healing workshops, brothers and sisters in Christ are always waiting to welcome us.

Loneliness can cause great emotional and physical wretchedness, but we should find total healing from loneliness when the communion of saints becomes a real element in our experience. It is a breathtaking concept. It extends not only into every part of the world but also into every age within human history. Mysteriously, we are called to know that we are one with Christians from the past and with Christians still to be born.

Even more mysteriously, in the communion of saints we reach out not only in space and time but beyond them into eternity. When I say my prayers for the healing of the world, I am not a lone voice crying in the wilderness. I join a great concourse. The apostle Paul is there; so is Francis of Assisi. So is my old grandfather, who was a Congregationalist lay preacher. So are the saints, martyrs and confessors from the whole of history, the high and the holy, the great and the good, those who have loved and will love the Lord from every shore and every age. When I sing in worship of God, I may not be much of a soloist, but what a back-up group I've got!

"Therefore we praise you, joining our voices with Angels and Archangels and with all the company of heaven, who for ever sing this hymn to proclaim the glory of your Name: Holy, holy, holy Lord, God of power and might, heaven and earth are full of your glory. Hosanna in the highest!" *(Book of Common Prayer).*

I believe in the forgiveness of sins. My sins would prevent me from joining in the prayers of heaven for the healing of the world, but the wonder is that, thanks to Jesus, my sins are forgiven. If you and I have received Jesus into our hearts as Savior and Lord, Healer and Friend, then across the dossier of our sins and stupidities is written the word *Forgiven.* We have already considered examples of the healing impact this can have on us, emotionally and physically. Think now how it enables and empowers us to be people of prayer.

"Lord, help me to live and pray within the freedom of your forgiveness. Liberate me to offer my sins, my sickness and my stress to be dissolved by your forgiving love. Liberate me from my grudges too, so that I in my turn may forgive those who have hurt me and mine. Liberate me from self-conscious embarrassment, that I may speak the gospel of forgiveness to those who have not yet heard it. Liberate me to pray, as you have commanded, for the healing of all who suffer. Lord, I am not worthy of any of this, but you are worthy enough for both of us!"

I believe in the resurrection of the body and the life everlasting. Amen. So we come to the end of the Apostles' Creed. And what a thought with which to finish! Other forms of healing are temporary and transient, but not Christian healing.

St. Athanasius writes, "Man is by nature afraid of death and the dissolution of the body, but the remarkable fact is that when he accepts the faith of the cross, he disregards this natural characteristic and through Christ loses his fear of death." Martin Luther exults, too, in this freedom from fear: "None has made himself master of terrors save Christ, who has conquered death and all temporal evils, even eternal death. Wherefore all who believe in him are no longer subject to fear but laugh at death with joyous assurance." For the Christian, the best is yet to be.

This afternoon, I went to a local hospital to visit an elderly parishioner who is suffering from what appears to be terminal cancer. As I sat by her bed, she spoke about her trust in Jesus and told me of an occasion many years ago when she was seriously ill and was prayed for by a former vicar. Unexpectedly, she had made a remarkable recovery. She was sure it was due to healing prayers.

She asked for prayer again, and I laid hands on her and focused the healing power of the Holy Trinity upon her. I have to say that this time I will be very surprised if she makes a physical recovery, and not at all surprised if she dies in the next few days. But it still seemed right to hold her hand and gently to urge her to "keep looking forward," because one of two things must happen. Against all the odds, there could be a new surge of life in this world—a miracle. Or, if she moves into death, and through death with her trust in Jesus, there will be a new surge of spiritual life for her in eternity. This, too, is a miracle, and either way, it is right to "keep looking forward."

The philosophy of Christian healing is always forward-looking. The difference Jesus makes begins here and now, and then goes on and on into the infinite mystery of heaven. Meditate now on how Charles Wesley expressed the eternal aspect of healing prayer in one of the greatest of all his hymns:

Finish then thy new creation;
Pure and spotless let us be;
Let us see thy great salvation,
Perfectly restored in thee;
Changed from glory into glory,
Till in heaven we take our place,
Till we cast our crowns before thee,
Lost in wonder, love and praise. Amen.

. . . Lost in wonder, love and praise.

[CHARLES WESLEY]

LEARNING TO PRAISE GOD

*T*he words that ended the last chapter take us to the heart of healing prayer. In fact, they take us to the heart of all prayer at its truest and deepest.

I have already quoted the words of Pope John Paul II: "We are an Easter people, and Hallelujah is our song." "Hallelujah" just means "Praise the Lord."

Praise is the most sublime form of prayer. It is also the kind of prayer that does us most good in body, mind and spirit. We neglect it at our peril.

This is why God wants us to praise him. It is not for his sake or for his benefit. God is not like those rather nauseating people who bolster their pride and fend off their insecurity by requiring the folks around them to feed them a diet of flattering praise. Our God knows that we need to praise him for *our* benefit. We damage ourselves if we do not praise and worship him.

Life provides many parallel experiences. It's important to appreciate excellence in every sphere. If I am blind to the beauty of nature when I walk through the countryside, if I never listen to really good music, if I never stretch myself by reading literature of quality—in short, if I am always satisfied with the superficial and the trivial, I do myself a great disservice.

It does *me* good to praise excellence, and it does *me* good to praise God, because it is good and beneficial and healing to appreciate the best.

Yet it is not always easy to appreciate the best. The best literature and music does stretch us, because it is complex and rich. Sometimes it's easier to appreciate the second-best, or even the third-rate, because it demands little of us.

Sinners that we are, the prayer of praise comes less naturally to us than the prayer of petition. It is so easy for prayer to degenerate into what my father used to call "an attack of the gimmes" ("Lord, gimme this, gimme that!"). It is far better for the center point of prayer to be the practice of the presence of God and the sense of healing awe and wonder that presence will bring.

As we come to the end of this book, I want to suggest not only that it's important to learn to deal with the various blocks, distractions and difficulties that we've considered in the earlier chapters, but also that we need to train ourselves to praise God regularly and imaginatively.

I believe there are three stages in the prayer of praise.

First, we need to select a personal "starter" for praise. Starters play an important role in life, for good or ill. Certain things act as starters for sin and evil. For instance, soft pornography or TV violence can start trains of thought which in turn lead to sick and destructive patterns of life and action. There are certain TV programs, films, magazines and books that it is better not to watch or read. But there are also starters for the good things in life. These springboards are invaluable aids in praising God.

Different starters will work for different people. Each of us must choose his or her own.

The "starter" may be an aspect of nature—perhaps the loveliness of a garden or the view from a mountaintop or a flower arrangement in church. If we do not happen to be in a garden or on a mountaintop or in church, a mental picture may well suffice. Or perhaps a photograph will help.

Or we may be led into the prayer of praise by the beauty of art. When my wife and I conducted a mission in Canada, we met a lady with a great talent for painting flowers. She photographed her own paintings and carried a few photos with her. She could give these lovely photos to her friends; also, in spare moments she could look at them herself and be led by them into the presence of God.

I have one of them on the desk in my study, and as I contemplate it now, I can feel the spirit of praise beginning to stir in me. Fine architecture or great music may have a similar effect.

Or the starter may be an aspect of spiritual beauty or truth— an incident from the life of Jesus or the life of one of the saints, or an evocative scriptural passage or hymn. There are examples in chapter nine.

Whatever our starter may be, it should lead us to the second stage in the prayer of praise, which is to attempt to express our feelings of praise in our own words. There should be no rush about this. As St. Teresa has said, "Hurry is the death of prayer." So stay with the starter as long as seems right, but then let the words flow just as they come and for as long as they come.

You can think the words silently or say them aloud. You can do it on your own or as part of a group. It is one of life's great experiences to be part of a group that has developed a genuine spirit of praise. Time can seem to stand still, as one person after another pours out his or her prayers of thanksgiving, praise and adoration.

But what happens if and when you run out of words? This is one of the great questions raised when one practices prayer in any depth, and it brings us to the third stage in our pattern of praising God.

When we run out of our own words, we are left with no alternative but to move into another prayer mode. We all have to decide which prayer mode is most appropriate for us personally.

Here are three possibilities.

We can move into liturgy, so that we are upheld by great prayers from the past. For instance, I sometimes find myself saying the great time-honored canticle known as the Te Deum:

We praise thee, O God: we acknowledge thee to be the Lord. All the earth doth worship thee, the Father everlasting. To thee all Angels cry aloud, the Heavens and all the Powers therein.

To Thee Cherubim and Seraphim continually do cry, Holy, Holy, Holy, Lord God of Hosts; Heaven and earth are full of the majesty of thy glory.

Thus my puny words are reinforced by greater words, and my

little mind is joined to the devotional life of greater souls.

You may have a favorite prayer that can do the same for you. St. Augustine, who wrote, "To praise God is the joy and happiness of the soul," has provided an abundant supply from which we can choose. For instance,

> Great art thou, O Lord, and greatly to be praised. Great is thy power, and thy wisdom is infinite. Thee would we praise without ceasing. Thou callest us to delight in thy praise, for thou hast made us for thyself, and our hearts find no rest till we rest in thee; to whom with the Father and the Holy Spirit all glory, praise and honor be ascribed, both now and evermore.

We have to know our prayer or canticle so well that we can say it without too much concentration or thought. Then our spirits can rest upon it, stand upon it and leap from it into new realms of praise.

A second possible prayer mode is that of total silence. I well remember George Bennett, who was one of the pioneers of the renewal of the Christian healing ministry in England. Before he took part in a healing service, he would sit in a corner of the church vestry practicing the prayer of silence. Around him there might be noise and bustle—choir members putting on their robes, the clergy checking last-minute details of the service—but George would be totally silent and detached. If you spoke to him, he might well not hear you. He had more important business as his soul stirred in silent praise. He called it "communing with the heavenlies." Maybe this could be your best prayer mode, too, when you move beyond words.

A third possible prayer mode is that of "tongues." My understanding and experience tell me that this is both a gift and an art—just as all prayer is. It involves abandoning our own words, letting sound flow from our lips and trusting God to impart to that sound whatever meaning he wills.

The use of this sort of prayer language when ordinary words have run out is becoming increasingly common in today's church. It is scriptural, and many people find it liberating. But it is not essential, and those who have not discovered tongues as a prayer mode should not be regarded as second-class Christians.

Whatever prayer mode you choose when you run out of words should be embarked upon without hurry. This prayer will be both an activity and a means of resting. It is an end in itself, because we were created to praise God, and it is also a means to an end. In fact, it is a means to several ends.

When the time is right, we shall find that praise moves us powerfully into other forms of prayer: a more cleansing experience of forgiveness, a more perceptive expression of thankfulness and a more effective ministry of intercession.

We will find ourselves commissioned and equipped afresh to live and love as Christians.

We will find that praising God is a royal road to happiness of spirit. Many people make the mistake of thinking that happiness can be sought and caught; actually, however, it eludes those who seek it and comes only as a by-product when minds and hearts are set on quite different courses.

Nothing is more likely to produce the by-product of happiness than the praise of God. Listen, for instance, to the bubbling happiness of the nineteenth-century Cornish evangelist Billy Bray as he speaks of his feelings as he praises God: "I can't help praising the Lord. As I go along the street, I lift up one foot and it seems to say 'Glory'; and I lift up the other and it seems to say 'Amen'; and so they keep up like that all the time I am walking."

The spirit of praise and the happiness it brings are a natural antidote to many of life's ills. In the final analysis, the best way to explore healing prayer is to respond to the biblical invitation, "Let everything that breathes praise the Lord!" Christians have the privilege of being absolutely honest to God about our hurts and grievances, our doubts and fears, but we also have the greater privilege of entering his healing presence and of worshiping him through Jesus Christ.

In the words of St. Augustine, then,

Look upon us, O Lord, and let the darkness of our soul vanish before the beams of thy brightness. Fill us with holy love, and open to us the treasures of thy wisdom. All our desire is known to thee; therefore perfect what thou hast begun and what thy Spirit has awakened us to ask in prayer. We seek thy face; turn thy face unto us and show us thy glory. Then shall our longing be satisfied and our peace shall be perfect; through Jesus Christ our Lord. Amen.